Comfort Island

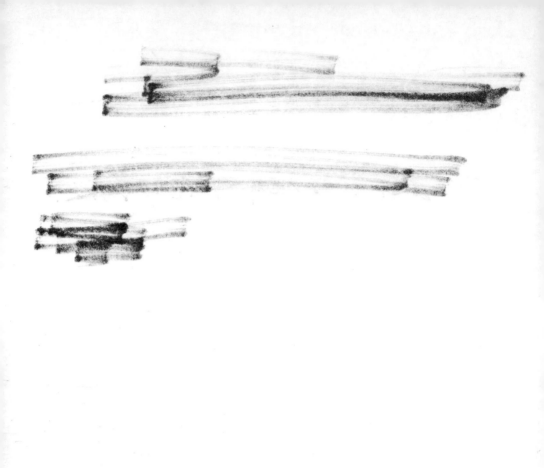

Comfort Island

One Family's Generational Journey

Tad Clark

ISBN: 1517091233
ISBN 13: 9781517091231
Library of Congress Control Number: 2015914227
CreateSpace Independent Publishing Platform
North Charleston, South Carolina

Table of Contents

Chapter 1   What Quirk of Fate Brought the Clarks to Comfort Island? ·1

Chapter 2   Running from the Sunset; Going East · · · · · · · · · · · · · · ·7

Chapter 3   Is One Car Enough for This Trip? · · · · · · · · · · · · · · 13

Chapter 4   Do We Have Lifejackets in the *Buzz?* · · · · · · · · · · 16

Chapter 5   What Happened to Our Impeccable Mansion? · · · · · · · ·22

Chapter 6   Let's Give the Town the Onceover · · · · · · · · · · · · ·25

Chapter 7   Mansions and the Shipping Channel · · · · · · · · · · · ·32

Chapter 8   Let's Go Ashore for a Firsthand Look · · · · · · · · · · ·37

Chapter 9   Will It Be Edgewood, Pine Tree or TI Club? · · · · · · · · · · ·44

Chapter 10 Could Pine Tree Take the Prize? · · · · · · · · · · · · · ·47

Chapter 11 Perhaps the TI Club Will Be the Top Choice · · · · · · · · · · ·50

Chapter 12 Let the Exploring Begin · · · · · · · · · · · · · · · · · ·52

Chapter 13 Alson S. Clark Left an Indelible Mark at Comfort Island ·55

Chapter 14 Where Are the Light Switches? · · · · · · · · · · · · · ·59

Chapter 15 Where Will We Sleep in this Big Old House? · · · · · · · · · · ·64

Chapter 16 Going Out to Eat Is Not as Simple as It Sounds · · · · · · · ·67

Chapter 17 Getting Acquainted With Island Inhabitants · · · · · · · · · ·70

Chapter 18 I Need Wheels of My Own · · · · · · · · · · · · · · · · ·73

Chapter 19 Hughie Papworth, the Flat, and Nemahbin Lodge · · · · · · ·78

Chapter 20 Fishing and Surveying the Territory Too · · · · · · · · · · ·81

Chapter 21 A Fishing Derby Papworth-style · · · · · · · · · · · · · ·85

Chapter 22 A Bat Hunt and Other Adventures With Hughie · · · · · · · ·87

Chapter 23 One Night at the Chalet Convinces Me · · · · · · · · · · ·91

Chapter 24 Comfort Island's Irreplaceable Gem –
the Front Porch ·95
Chapter 25 A "Commanding View"· ·100
Chapter 26 We Need a Reliable Boat · · · · · · · · · · · · · · · · · · ·103
Chapter 27 The Beach, Makeshift Docking, and
Evenings at Comfort ·107
Chapter 28 A Few More Memories of My First Summer · · · · · · · · · 111
Chapter 29 Indian Lore, Tour Boats, Modernization · · · · · · · · · · · 117
Chapter 30 Hughie, Boating, Island Romance· · · · · · · · · · · · · · ·122
Chapter 31 The Dining Porch; Another Comfort Island Gem · · · · · · ·126
Chapter 32 Relatives, Houseguests and the *MT* · · · · · · · · · · · · · ·132
Chapter 33 Exploring the River ·136
Chapter 34 Making New Friends and Water-skiing· · · · · · · · · · · · ·139
Chapter 35 How About a Row? ·142
Chapter 36 The First Restoration Continues · · · · · · · · · · · · · · · ·146
Chapter 37 Venturing Forth at Night· ·150
Chapter 38 The Great Blue Heron Adventure · · · · · · · · · · · · · · ·152
Chapter 39 What's My Line? ·155
Chapter 40 Let's Go Cruisin' ·158
Chapter 41 Leg Two of the Grand Tour: Beauharnois Locks,
Montreal & the Ottawa River · · · · · · · · · · · · · · · · · ·164
Chapter 42 The Rideau Canal Leg of the Grand Tour· · · · · · · · · · ·168
Chapter 43 Notable Canine Characters· · · · · · · · · · · · · · · · · · · 174
Chapter 44 Romance ·178
Chapter 45 Want to Hit a Few? ·182
Chapter 46 Making My Vocation My Vacation· · · · · · · · · · · · · · ·187
Chapter 47 The Unpaid Help· ·192
Chapter 48 The Full Catastrophe· ·197
Chapter 49 Is It a Picnic or a Shore dinner?· · · · · · · · · · · · · · · ·200
Chapter 50 A Bump in the Road ·204
Chapter 51 Mom Called It Her "Mad Room" · · · · · · · · · · · · · · ·208
Chapter 52 The Joys of Dog Rearing· ·212
Chapter 53 The "Home Depot" Restoration Program · · · · · · · · · · ·216

Chapter 54 First, Let's Check With the Amish · · · · · · · · · · · · · · · · · · ·223
Chapter 55 "It Was the Best of Times" ·226
Chapter 56 "Brooklyn," Our First Good Dog · · · · · · · · · · · · · · · ·232
Chapter 57 "It Was the Worst of Times" · · · · · · · · · · · · · · · · · · ·235
Chapter 58 Moving On ·238
Chapter 59 Want a Great Location and a Project Too? · · · · · · · · · · ·241
Chapter 60 Can an Island Have Nine Lives? · · · · · · · · · · · · · · · · ·244
Chapter 61 *Moonrise Kingdom* ·248
Chapter 62 The Zooks Have Landed ·251
Chapter 63 The Search For a New Steward Continues · · · · · · · · · · ·254
Chapter 64 How Do You Clear Out a Mansion? · · · · · · · · · · · · · · · ·258
Chapter 65 Buried Treasures ·263
Chapter 66 "River Rats" ·266
Chapter 67 How Does One Say Goodbye to a Place so Dear? · · · · · ·268

✿

CHAPTER 1

What Quirk of Fate Brought the Clarks to Comfort Island?

"I LOVE THIS old black and white photo of Comfort Island, Dad. The four-story house is up on top of the hill. The beach, docks, boathouse, and boats are close enough to touch."

Someday we'll travel east and spend a summer at Comfort Island, Tad."

The picture hung next to Dad's secretary-style antique desk in his Montecito office. The desk had belonged to his father and featured a pullout-writing surface and pigeon hole compartments built into the area behind the writing surface for stowing letters and other documents. The office was located a short distance from our home in Santa Barbara, California. I visited Dad's office once or twice a week during the mid-1950s to say, "Hello" or more often in search of a couple of dollars to satisfy my voracious appetite at the San Ysidro Pharmacy.

I generally got a short speech about not ruining my appetite before dinner, or questioning why I couldn't find a snack at home. I listened respectfully waiting for the sermon to end then preceded quickly via my bike the short distance to the café. I turned ten in 1956, the year my father turned forty-eight.

Dad stood up and joined me for a closer look at the 1885 photo of Comfort Island. He took a magnifying glass from the desktop to assist our inspection. Dad went bald before the age of thirty and he wore a moustache for most of his married life. I noted that even at this relatively young age he had a stooped posture. I knew he was six-feet tall but he seldom stretched himself to anywhere near that height. His hair had not turned gray yet, but he looked older than his age.

I pointed to the picture and said, "Look at the steam yacht. Some sort of mist is coming from that valve on top of the cabin next to the smokestack. What's that?"

"It is probably Captain Comstock blowing the steam whistle on the *Mamie C.*"

I am a member of the fourth generation of the Clark ownership of Comfort Island. The photo looking up at the house was a fixture on my dad's wall for many years and now it hangs on my wall in Asheville, North Carolina. My great grandfather, Alson Ellis Clark commissioned a series of photographs in the 1880s leaving behind a pictorial record of those early days. He was born in Barre, Vermont, in 1838 and moved to Chicago in 1863.

AE Clark

Few written records from the A.E. Clark (1838 – 1911) days have survived but I did find an account in *Chicago: Its History and Its Builders* by Josiah Currey that provides both factual and character details. My second cousin Edwin Hill Clark II compiled a detailed genealogy of the Clarks as well.

Josiah Curry provides clues and insight into Great Grandfather Clark's character and personality when he says, "his good works do follow him. While he prospered through the capable management and intelligent direction of important business affairs his success was a source of gratification to him not because of the position which it gave him in commercial circles but because of the opportunity which it afforded him to aid his fellowmen and to further all projects which are intended for the betterment of mankind…He was a lover of music and possessed a fine voice. For fifteen years he was the tenor singer in the Second Universalist church, in which he long held membership."

A.E. Clark left home in New Hampshire at age sixteen and worked in the hat manufacturing business at Bent & Bush in Boston until the outbreak of the Civil War. He joined the Forty-Fifth Volunteer army regiment in 1861 for a nine-month assignment. At the completion of his service period, he began moving west. He arrived in Chicago in 1863 where he worked as a commission merchant until 1871 when he became a member of the Chicago Board of Trade.

He married Sarah Skinner in 1869. Her father had a business making miner's lamps in Racine, Wisconsin. Her mother died when she was twenty-one and she moved to Chicago to live with her aunt, Sarah Talcott, and her uncle, Mancel Talcott. Her father excelled at inventions but failed as a businessperson.

Alson and Sarah had four children together. Mary Emily was the only girl. She was the first-born in 1870 and became known as Mamie. My grandfather, Mancel, was born in 1874 followed by Alson Skinner Clark in 1876 and Edwin in 1878.

Sarah Skinner Clark & Mary Emily Clark

As a successful businessman, A.E. Clark had the means to take his family and servants on vacation during the summer months. Their vacation spot of choice in the years through 1880 was Old Point Comfort, Virginia, but in 1881 Mamie died of diphtheria. Family lore as reported by my dad, contends that Great Grandmother Clark said, "I'll never go back to Old Point Comfort to relive my heartache again." Hence, the A.E. Clark family began their search for a new summer headquarters.

In 1882 the Clarks went to visit the Edwin Hill family who were friends from Chicago. The Hills had a summer cottage in the 1000 Islands of northern New York. The family rode the train to Gananoque, Ontario, Canada and journeyed the last fifteen miles to the Hill's residence on

Wauwinet Island by boat. The 1000 Islands run along a fifty-mile corridor of southern Ontario, Canada and the New York border beginning where Lake Ontario ends. The Hills resided on the New York side near Alexandria Bay. The Clarks liked being on the water and boating too. Great Grandfather Clark purchased the island adjacent to the Hill's during their stay, and so began the Clark tenure on Comfort Island.

1880s with windmill

The 1000 Islands area had gained notoriety in 1872 after train magnate, George Pullman of Pullman sleeping-car fame, invited President Ulysses S. Grant to visit his island. The Thousand Islands Sun newspaper reports that Grant, his family, and General Phillip Sheridan "roughed it at Pullman's Camp Charming for five days...The presidential sojourn advertised the 1000 Islands to the country, and almost overnight this area turned into a famous resort. No longer was this merely a sportsman's paradise." The press corps that accompanied the president's visit posted accounts of the beauty and physical splendor they experienced during their stay. The response to these articles was exactly what Mr. Pullman intended.

The 1000 Islands became a vacation destination for people of means. Susan W. Smith says in her manuscript *The History of Recreation in the 1000 Islands*, "The railroads built sidings to Clayton and Cape Vincent and as many as twenty trains a day would come and go at the village stations."

Magnificent hotels were built throughout the island chain. Those of greater wealth, like my great grandfather, began building cottages on a number of the 1800 islands. Soon a small fleet of steam yachts carrying successful islanders toured the river to visit neighbors or simply to be seen.

CHAPTER 2

—— ∝ ——

Running from the Sunset; Going East

IN 1961, DAD recognized that Betsy's high school graduation presented an opportunity for the whole family to convene on the East coast for the summer. I was scheduled to enter a boarding school in Maine in the fall. Spending the summer in New York meant Dad could drive me to Hebron Academy when the new school year began in September.

"You mean we're actually going to Comfort Island after all these years of talking about it?" I asked Dad.

"Yes, Tad, I finally sold your mother on the idea. We will attend Betsy's graduation from Miss Hall's School in Massachusetts then drive to Alexandria Bay to spend the summer on Comfort Island."

I thought back to the day in 1956 when my dad and I scanned the 1885 photo of Comfort Island with the magnifying glass. I wondered then and for the five years that followed if we would ever make the trip there as he promised. My older sister, Betsy, had visited Comfort Island briefly with Mom and Dad in 1948 after completing first grade, but my other sister, Deborah, was only one at the time, and I was two. We weren't invited to go. Instead, we stayed home in California with a very sweet nanny named Field.

I have Dad's diaries dating from 1960-1975, which allows me to record these early years with greater accuracy. Each diary covers a five-year span. The leather bound journals are six inches high and four-and-one-half inches wide. There are four lines allotted for recording the events for each of the five years. Dad was quite proficient at packing many details into each day's entry.

Deborah and my mom took the train East for Betsy's graduation. Dad and I drove the 1960 white Mercury Commuter station wagon to meet them in Pittsfield, Massachusetts.

My excitement was so great that I hardly slept the night before we left. I had completed my school exams, but I was going to miss the eighth-grade graduation ceremony, which only added to my jubilation. Each member of my class faced the daunting prospect of presenting an original solo performance of their own invention.

Traveling with Dad was always a challenge because he took a long time each day to get up to speed. Indeed, we rarely got on the road before noon. He relished sleeping-in and when he did get up, he puttered around at an agonizingly slow pace. "I've got to shave...I've got to get some breakfast (about noon)...I need to use the john, Tad, and I can't rush that." This routine was so ingrained that not even the excitement of embarking on the trip could jar Dad from his habitual pattern.

He always left his packing to the last minute and this trip was no exception. He had just a few last minute preparations to take care of before we could get on the road that first day. A trip to his office to collect business papers was first on his list even though he seldom let a day go by when he didn't go to his office after eating lunch out. Next he needed to get maps of our potential routes since it had slipped his mind for the preceding three months. This represented the height of procrastination since Dad had anything but a busy schedule.

In his rush getting home from the auto club to pack, he got a speeding ticket. By the time the car was finally packed and the road trip East was actually ready to commence, it was 1:30 in the afternoon. We clicked-off the first five miles of the three thousand mile trek before Dad spotted one of his favored luncheon restaurants and said, "I need to stop for lunch. I didn't have time to eat with all the work I had to do this morning."

It was nice to start the trip off with a chuckle, and I freely admit we shared many more laughs before we reached our destination. We made it all the way to Victorville, California the first day or one hundred and fifty-eight miles. I did a quick calculation and figured it would take us a little more than twenty days at our present pace to cover the necessary three thousand miles. Unfortunately, we had only one week to make it from Victorville to Pittsfield. We were behind schedule beginning with day one.

Dad drove to Las Vegas where we had lunch. I had never been any further East than this, and I scrutinized the maps to get an idea of where we were headed next. Just how far we had to go hadn't computed with Dad yet, and I recall he let me drive several hours during the first few days on the sparsely traveled roads of Nevada, Utah, and Colorado.

Dad had obtained maps and "triptiks" for our journey. Triptiks had their start in 1911 and still exist today in the twenty-first century. These handy travel guides consist of mini-maps covering short stretches of road bound into a booklet. The traveler flips each page forward from a spiral binding at the top of the booklet for the next section of road as they advance on their trip. Things like construction, mileage, rest stops, and terrain characteristics are included. Dad and Mom loved them. We had to decide whether to take the scenic route through Steamboat Springs, Grand Lake and Rocky Mountain National Park or the faster northern route the auto club recommended. It was an easy choice. We took the slower, scenic route.

We stayed in motels that conjure images of romantic western settings. In Vernal, Utah we stayed at the Red Cloud Lodge; at Grand Lake, Colorado it was the Western Brands Motel; and in Ames, Iowa the Silver Saddle Motel. I checked "Card Cow" for a second look and all of our stops featured one-story buildings with occupant parking in front of each room. A swimming pool was a standard frill at each of our stops.

Dad kept good notes of the fun we had the first five days. I swam at the Red Cloud, we played miniature golf at Grand Lake, and had a snowball fight at 12,000 feet while passing through Rocky Mountain National Park.

I remember the setting for our snowball fight with some detail. We had pulled off at one of the overlooks above the tree line. There were patches of snow and a grassy area that led to a steep slope. I walked to the edge of the steeper section where I was greeted by a white Rocky Mountain Goat coming my way. The goat didn't seem too concerned until a younger boy became too animated for the wild critter's taste and as quickly as it appeared it disappeared. I followed the goat to a spot where I could see down the slope, but it had vanished. I felt quite fortunate to have seen such a rare and timid creature at close range.

We had averaged about three hundred miles a day for the first five days, which meant we'd have to nearly double our current pace for the final three days. On the first day of our three-day driving marathon we got on the road at 11:30 after Dad overslept, which he notated in his diary entry for June 10th. Dad intended to make up time by getting an earlier start. We traveled late covering 440 miles before stopping for the night in Ames, Iowa well after dark. Arriving late in the evening presented a different sort of problem. Restaurants serving credible meals generally closed at seven-thirty or eight, and what you got after that was up for grabs.

I have a clear memory of the diner in Ames where we ate that night. It was the only place still serving dinner, and there was no name to the café only a neon sign shaped like an arrow pointing at the doorway with the word "Eat" illuminated. A thorough inspection of this joint was unnecessary. Several farmers were drinking coffee at the counter facing a soda fountain and two other men were sitting at a table across the room looking disheveled and worn from what we surmised was too much celebrating. A quick look at the faded chintz curtains and the oilcloth tablecloth that made a greasy plate look clean by comparison convinced me to order the peanut butter and jelly sandwich with extra chips. Dad must have been groggy from all the driving because he ordered the $1.29 T-bone steak. Dad was not blessed with good teeth and taking-on that steak was like a mismatch in a 15-round main-event prizefight. The outcome was never in question with gristle scoring a TKO over what we thought might be steak. The battle was mercifully halted before any teeth were lost.

The two of us were showing signs of fatigue even though the trip was only a little over half over with only two days to go. At dinner that night, we got laughing and couldn't stop as we imagined Dad's steak dinner being peeled off the bumper of some truck that clobbered "Ol' Bessy" out on the road a week or two before our arrival.

The following morning Dad was up at 7:00 and we got our first early start. However Dad's diary says it all, "hard Sunday drive thru Iowa traffic." The further East we went the more congested the highways became, which slowed our progress even more. Roads typically went right through the middle of every town and city along the way. Local residents used the same road as we did. These folks had no knowledge or appreciation that we had a deadline to meet thousands of miles away while they dawdled along enjoying conversation and the sunny weather.

I knew Dad was feeling stressed as he contended with the snarled traffic because his two nervous driving mannerisms were on display. He was moving the steering wheel back and forth in a short arc that is similar to a child filling in an open space with a crayon, and he lightly tugged at his lower ear lobes with his thumb and index finger.

Constructions on future highways that would facilitate more efficient travel going forward were currently of little help. Trucks, farm equipment, and Sunday drivers generated many delays throughout the day. When we reached the Chicago area, four-lane toll roads became an option, and we took them. We made it to Toledo, Ohio at 1:30 a.m. after covering 595 miles for by far our longest mileage day.

The last day was the craziest of all. We hit thunderstorms near Utica, New York, and I remember vividly sharing hysterical laughter with Dad at 2 a.m. when we lost our way in some residential Massachusetts neighborhood. We got laughing after we realized that we had circled around and were passing the same houses for a second time. I suggested knocking on some stranger's door to ask for directions. In traditional fashion, we drove the final 677 miles on our eighth and final travel day to make it to the Wagon Wheel Motel at 3 a.m. Miraculously Dad got up and met the train carrying Mom and Deb five hours later that same morning.

CHAPTER 3

⚭

Is One Car Enough for This Trip?

"HOW IN THE world are we going to fit all these suitcases into the back of this station wagon, Mancel?" Mom asked Dad.

"You married an architect, Ellen. I made a living figuring out how to make things fit into tight spaces."

"I'll help get the suitcases stowed in the back, Dad, but you're going to need a periscope to see anything coming up behind us," I said.

I don't recall how many suitcases we had in all, but I packed light and only had one medium-sized bag. Dad had a full-sized leather suitcase that he used for decades. It folded at the bottom like a book and had two compartments resembling drawers with rounded corners for stowing clothes. A semi-flexible divider panel fit over each compartment and was kept in place with turnbutton fasteners that are commonly used to secure removable canvas. The two sides folded together and snapped shut at the top where a handle was attached for carrying the valise.

My sister, Deb, accompanied Mom to Pittsfield via train, and her recollection is that they had at least four suitcases in tow. Apparently the prospect of being sequestered at Comfort Island for the summer had Mom preparing for any eventuality. Betsy was assuredly traveling light since Miss Hall's School mandated uniforms and only allowed each student to possess a maximum of three civilian outfits. I surmise we had a minimum of seven suitcases to squeeze into the rear cargo area.

Typical of cars from that era was the exaggerated tail fins that swooped up and out to the side, and an abundance of chrome trim that ran the length of the sides at door-handle height. Distinctive dual head-lights protruded from a recessed chrome grill, and fender ornaments resembling miniature anti-aircraft machine-gun sights had been positioned over each set of lights.

An extra large, rectangular speedometer housing dominated the instrument panel. A chrome horn-blowing apparatus was attached to the center of the steering wheel, but the top third of what would have been a circle was deleted to provide better visibility for the gauges.

We tried loading the suitcases upright first and then we laid the bigger satchels flat. It was like a puzzle, and I remember we had to load the final few contents from the back seat since nothing more would fit through the back window.

As I predicted, the view out the back window was totally blocked. I really hoped there would be no reason to slam on the brakes, or we'd all be sitting in a sea of suitcases.

I also checked to see if the front wheels were off the ground with so much weight in the back. I wanted to be sure so I tried lifting the front end, but it didn't budge so I figured we were good to go.

The seven-day trip to Massachusetts with Dad was comfortable and relaxed compared to this circus. I braced myself for a seven-hour ride in an industrial trash compactor.

"Mom, I've kind of gotten used to the front seat on the trip from California. Can I sit up there?"

"Not on your life, Sonny-boy."

"OK, but I dibs the window seat behind Dad."

Deb surveyed the situation from the passenger-side rear door with her hands on her hips then she narrowed her eyes and said, "I suppose as the youngest, I get stuck in the middle?"

I had already slid into the seat next to the window behind where Dad would be driving, and I knew what Betsy was about to say as if I was a master of mental telepathy, "You got the middle, Deborah. That's how it goes."

We hadn't been driving an hour before Deb started in, "I don't like it in the middle and how come you didn't get air-conditioning when you bought this crummy car, Daddy? It's hot and sticky in here. Will we be there soon?"

Even next to the open window, I felt heat radiating from the asphalt roadway. Deb, Betsy and I sang refrains from a couple of traditional folk jingles that were popular with kids taking long car trips during this time period. The songs have repetitive lyrics and are easy to remember. Best of all they helped to pass the time. We started with "Found a Peanut, which was rotten, but I ate it anyway, just now. I got ill, called a doctor, had an operation, but died anyway," and on and on to the tune of Clementine. Tiring of that sweet ballad we moved on to "99 bottles of beer on the wall, 99 bottles of beer, if one of those bottles should happen to fall, 98 bottles on the wall." The object is keep eliminating beers one refrain at a time until zero is reached, but I recall that the heat eroded our enthusiasm and eventually we simply lapsed into silence.

All of us were ready to cheer out loud as we drove between the cement pillars that supported the "Welcome to Alexandria Bay" sign. I had never been here before and I was excited to arrive after years of anticipation.

"Where is the Island? Can we see it from here?" I asked.

"It's about a mile upriver, Son. We'll have to get a boat to take a look," Dad said.

"Are we going to see it today?" Deb asked.

Dad said, "That depends on Mancel Root who is doing the caretaking for us now. He was going to try to get the *Buzz* running, but the boat is old and hasn't been run much for quite some time."

CHAPTER 4

— ✂ —

Do We Have Lifejackets in the *Buzz*?

THE WELCOME ARCH spanned the two lanes and looked sturdy enough to drive a tank across. The rest of Church Street continues a half-a-mile or so from the sign to James Street and the middle of the village. This street and many of the adjoining side streets conjured up images of a quaint New England town with a profusion of oaks and maples surrounding well kept, two story, wooden-framed houses. The Village maintained a strip of grass between the curb and the sidewalks that run parallel to the street on both sides. The areas close to the houses typically displayed neatly trimmed scrubs and flowers.

"I'm ready to get checked into our motel then the rest of you can do whatever you want until dinnertime," Mom said.

We turned left at Crossman Street midway between the arch and downtown and proceeded to the Maple Crest Motel.

It was after five when we finished checking-in, which was a good thing because Mr. Root was only a part-time caretaker but had a full time job refinishing boats at Hutchinson's Boat Works. His workday had ended at the same time we got to town. Consequently he was available to help us attempt to get the *Buzz* running. Mr. Root's son, Wilford, and Wilford's wife, Kay, owned the Maple Crest adding to the convenience and family atmosphere. The Motel's location was just up the street from Otter Creek and Wilford's dock where *Buzz* was tied up.

Kay called her father-in-law to let him know we had arrived. While we waited, my dad, Wilford, and I chatted in the motel parking lot.

Dad had designed the motel addition during 1958. In 1933, he graduated from Yale University with an architectural degree. Most all of Dad's architectural career had been restricted to Pasadena or Santa Barbara, California except this project that he did for the Roots.

I knew Dad mostly designed houses, and I was pretty sure he'd taken on this assignment as a personal favor and the challenge of trying something different. A row of multiple units was attached to the back of the original house. Units at ground level ran adjacent to a parking area and perpendicular to the street. A second row of units overhead mirrored those below. A Monterey style, cantilevered upper walkway extended the length of the second floor and an overhanging roof sheltered the upper porch area from the elements.

Wilford said, "Gee, Mr. Clark, you sent us the plans but you never got to see how everything fit together till now. It has worked out great for us. The motel business supplements the income I earn working at the Uncle Sam Boat Tours and we make a comfortable living for ourselves and our daughter, Wendy."

"The builder did a swell job. It's hard to tell where they added the new section on. And Wilford, please call me Mancel. Mr. Clark makes me feel like I've skipped ahead to being a senior citizen," Dad said.

I recognized the second floor Monterey porch design because when Dad added on to our board-and-batten farmhouse in Santa Barbara, he added an overhanging wooden porch to the second level there too. I always liked the look and I found it a fine place to sit and relax.

All-weather aluminum chairs and accent tables outside each room at Maple Crest was likewise an invitation to sit a spell and enjoy the tranquil setting.

The office and living quarters for the Root family were included in the older two-story, wooden structure. The white house with green trim mirrored the style of the houses I'd seen coming into town. It had several pitches to the roofline that made the building stand out. A spacious, screened front porch faced the street and a front door led to the registration desk.

My excitement level was so high with the prospect of finally getting to Comfort Island that I took little notice of the family quarters or the warm reception extended to us by Kay and Wilford.

"Here comes Dad," Wilford said.

Sure enough a slightly built fellow with short white hair pulled up on his three-wheeled bicycle. A large wire basket was attached to the front handlebars. His skin was nearly the color of his hair. He appeared to be one of those people who are all but allergic to the sun. Despite his slender stature, he had a spark in his eye that suggested energy. I had a sense that he was wiry and far from frail.

I don't remember too much about Wilford, but he and his dad were both relatively short compared to Dad's six-foot height. I also remember that Wilford had a huskier build than his dad.

It seemed odd when Dad said, "Good to see you, Mancel."

And it made me laugh when Mr. Root said, "Good to see you too, Mancel."

They made a bow to each other and we all chuckled together. Back in 1900 when Mancel Root was born, it was a common practice for local folks to name a new member of their family after the summer residents who provided jobs for the townspeople. Mancel Root's uncle, George Root, was the original Comfort Island caretaker starting work for the family in 1883. He stayed at his caretaking position until his death in 1953. Someone in Clark family sent him a check every month for seventy years. Mancel had been named after my grandfather, Mancel Sr.

George Root and Mom

"It's only about a block to my dock where *Buzz* is. We can all walk down and have a look," Wilford said.

"I'll get Deb. I know she wants to come too," I said.

The photo of *Buzz* that hung on Dad's wall in Santa Barbara had been taken in 1926 with Dad at the wheel. The majestic craft he drove on that occasion was in stark contrast with the rundown relic the boat had become thirty-five years later. The white paint on the sides was chipped and faded. The varnish was blistering. The windshield and most of the front deck were no longer part of the boat. What happened?

After George Root passed away, Dad had told me that Mancel had taken over the caretaking responsibilities. I hadn't realized until Dad told me that evening that Mancel wanted a boat he could move around in so he cut eight feet of varnished, wooden deck away to make more room for fishing. In addition to fishing he had also been using *Buzz* to occasionally check on Comfort.

A local boat builder named Louis Kenyon built *Buzz* in 1910 and my grandfather took delivery that summer. The 1910 style boat was long and slender. *Buzz* is twenty-four feet long and only five feet wide at its widest point. A sharply pointed bow with a bronze shield know as a "cutwater" served to assist the craft as it cut through waves rather than slap the bottom of the boat while skipping over the top of the water. Reaching speeds great enough to plane a boat hadn't even been considered in 1910.

Standard construction material was wood when *Buzz* was built and fiberglass powerboats were still in their infancy in 1961. The sides were painted while the decks and interior were varnished.

Crossman Street ended where a crude boat-launching ramp continued under the water's surface. Wilford's docks were located next to the ramp. They were floating docks with buoyant material affixed underneath the wooden decking. Brackets were attached to the side of the dock in ten-foot intervals. Posts were driven into the mud at the river bottom while being held in place by the brackets. The posts kept the docks in place and acted as a handy convenience for keeping one's balance when climbing in or out of boats docked there.

Dad and Mancel climbed into the *Buzz* to see about getting her started, but water sloshed over the floorboards from the bilge as soon as they got in.

"I've got a hand pump here on the rack I use for my fishing gear," Mancel said.

The pump was a cleverly designed apparatus consisting of a five-foot section of round downspout gutter-pipe made of tin with a funnel-like mouth connected with solder at the top. A second section of pipe was connected below the funnel-shaped top perpendicular to the upright pipe. A stick with a handle at the top and a diaphragm at the bottom pulled water up the tube where it exited through the second pipe over the side of the boat.

Mancel removed one of the floorboards revealing about eight inches of water. He submerged the pump and began the up and down motion. Sure enough, water flowed out the perpendicular pipe and back into the river.

I marveled at the simple efficiency of this pumping system, and as the water level in the bilge was drawing down Dad said, "Tad, you might as well get in here and finish the job so you know how to do it. I have a feeling this will become one of your daily chores this summer."

I had been looking at the boat from the dock, but once I got inside I noticed more details. The boat tapered to a point in the bow and narrowed to a bench seat wide enough for two in the stern. Mid-ship was the widest point where another bench seat was secured to the boat frame with screws. This seat was wide enough for three people of moderate size. A wooden lever was affixed to the starboard side of the boat next to the middle seat for steering. Pushing the lever forward turned the boat to the left and pulling it back turned it to the right.

Mancel Root had inserted a new battery before we arrived, which was a good thing because even though the motor was not the original, it was nonetheless old and worn out. The starter groaned as it labored to turn the motor over. It was slow grinding at first and then the grinding got faster until it sputtered to life. The motor coughed and threatened to quit several times, but after a few minutes it began running a little smoother. Dusk was closing in by the time *Buzz* was as ready to go. Dad drove and Deb and I sat next to him as we pulled away from the floating dock. I had some experience boating in California but that was mostly sailing. Power boating was a whole new experience for me, and I was plenty excited about just about everything to do with being on the water in the 1000 Islands. We advised Wilford, "Send out a search party if we aren't back in forty-five minutes."

CHAPTER 5

ॐ

What Happened to Our Impeccable Mansion?

I WAS SITTING next to the gunwale where it was easy to look over the side into the bluish-green water where I noticed weeds growing toward the surface from the murky bottom. Watching the water go by and focusing on the bow and the plume of water that crested on each side of the cutwater creating tiny waves made me feel as though we were going much faster than five or six miles per hour. The *Buzz* felt a little unstable as it rolled excessively when waves hit the boat from the side. I realized that the narrowness of the hull, and the mostly rounded bottom were to blame for such exaggerated tipping.

We taxied out of the bay where Wilford's docks were located. On the same side of the bay as Wilford's dock were six or eight large wooden boathouses. These belonged to various boating concerns. Some were rental boathouses where individuals could rent a seasonal slip. Other boathouses like Hutchinson's Boat Works, where Mancel Root worked, were in the boat building and restoration business. On the far side of the bay were three or four private cottages with attending docks and boathouses.

After a few hundred yards the River began to widen out, and on the right I saw the Alexandria Bay Town Dock extending from the main street downtown a hundred yards or more in our direction. To my left loomed the impressive Edgewood Resort with several docks and an assortment of runabouts and cruisers tied up there. Up on the hill behind the docks was a large motel complex with oversize plate glass windows providing expansive views of the river from the dining room. I knew it was the dining room because I could see folks eating behind those windows.

I wasn't quite sure what course the ships followed, and I asked Dad, "Where is the shipping channel from here, and how often do ships go through? I haven't seen one yet."

He pointed to an area beyond the island immediately to our right and said, "The main shipping channel is about a quarter of a mile over there. I'm not too sure how much traffic the seaway sees now that it has been expanded for bigger ships. We'll find out when we move into Comfort."

I knew this was where the giant freighters moved goods to major cities in the Midwest and Eastern North American. I'd heard about the St Lawrence Seaway and there it was. I saw the shapes of channel markers, grand houses and island outlines in the distance. I was curious to take a look, but Dad said, "I think we'd better follow this inside channel past the Edgewood just in case the old engine conks out."

Everything was kind of a blur for me at that point as we passed several islands with more grand houses and boathouses, and numerous rock outcroppings scattered about in unlikely places. Three or four houses we passed were three stories high, and obviously had been built generations ago. It was starting to get dark, which made details harder to see. Ironically, this passageway would become familiar enough to paint from memory in the years to come after hundreds of trips over this same route.

We passed between two islands where I could feel the stern fishtailing as the boat battled a swift oncoming current that affected the steering and the direction of our course. As I looked over the side of the boat, I saw small whirlpools, which was proof of the water pushing its way through this narrow cut. I was beginning to regard *Buzz* as a craft, I'd rather avoid if I knew we'd be encountering rough seas.

From the head of these two islands another island appeared about four hundred yards ahead. About half way there, I recognized the outline of the Comfort Island house. I asked, "Can we land and go have a look?"

Dad said, "It's too late to attempt a landing tonight," but we idled off the beach, near where the picture of the steam yacht blowing the whistle was taken. I gazed up at the big old house, but it was too dark to make out details. Dad held his head high and the way he smiled convinced me that he was reminiscing about treasured memories.

I glanced at Deb as my eyes widened and my pursed lips reflected a smile communicating disbelief. Deb mimicked my expression, and I knew she had similar thoughts as me. While I'd been told that the magnificent cupola was torn off after a lightening strike in 1948, I hadn't imagined how ghostly it would make the house appear. I harkened back to what the Buzz looked like in my memory compared to what I saw today. And now I saw the shell of a house that I imagined being a castle.

CHAPTER 6

∞

Let's Give the Town the Onceover

I WAS THE second one up. Betsy was off walking. I took the lull as an opportunity to enhance my familiarity with a convenient porch chair while I scrutinized the New York Times sports section. It was the previous day's sports section but being from the West Coast, I found it quite interesting to consider an East Coast point of view. Around eight-thirty Betsy returned from her walk and Deborah was up by then too. We conferred on the balcony about what to do while we waited for Dad.

Betsy was her typical dynamic self, and she suggested we tour the downtown, which she had passed in her morning constitutional. I watched her as she put her right hand on her hip and frowned saying, "Well when do you suppose Daddy-o will be ready to get moving? You two may not care but it drives me crazy waiting like this."

Deb rolled her eyes and looked toward the sky as she said, "You know Dad. It won't be early."

To quell the growing mutiny I said, "I cast my vote for the tour of downtown."

Betsy was fidgeting while Deb stretched her arms up and then sideways as if gearing up to take flight.

"Let's go," Betsy said.

We started up the sidewalk toward Church Street. I watched as Betsy took off like an Olympic speed-walker. I followed along but when I looked to see where Deb was, she had stopped at the yard next to the motel to admire their flowers. Betsy stopped at the end of the block where Crossman and Church Street intersect. By the time Deb sauntered up to

Betsy and me, Betsy had both hands on her hips by this time as she said, "Come on. Can't you move any faster than that, Deborah?"

I looked to the right up Church Street and saw the welcome arch a couple of blocks away where we had entered Alexandria Bay the previous evening. We turned the opposite direction and continued walking down Church Street toward the downtown.

Deb and Betsy walked together a few yards ahead of me. While I followed, I pondered our individual family attributes. I fell a couple of inches short of growing to Dad's height of six feet, but Deb and Betsy were both very close to five-foot-two, and I knew Mom was shorter yet and barely five feet tall. I marveled at how quickly Betsy covered ground even though I was considerably taller. How could she and Deb be so different I wondered?

Deb was a dawdler and had earned the nickname of "Pokey" for getting left behind at the Santa Barbara beach one day. They looked alike to someone who didn't see them often, but they had many opposite traits in reality. I could easily detect bigger bones and a larger frame on Deb as they moved down the sidewalk. Indeed, Betsy had finer bones and features. Deb had a deep tan on her arms and legs whereas Betsy had very fair skin and showed no tan at all. They both had brown hair but I knew Betsy's eyes were more hazel and Deb's were brown.

Deb and I were only a year apart whereas Betsy was four years older than me. I was an unwelcome addition to the family from Betsy's perspective. All of a sudden she was not the center of Mom and Dad's attention every minute of the day. She hurled my toy police car at me when I was two or three and left a scar over my eye that set the tone for an antagonistic relationship that was still smoldering.

Deb and I were closer but not that close either. Deb and I lost rapport after Mom and Dad decided that they would put her in charge when they went out for the evening. I was more than a year older and it didn't go well with me when she'd call them to report that I'd gone off to see my girlfriend.

We crested the hill at a fast saunter as we reached the beginning of the commercial district. Betsy said something like, "Well here it is folks – downtown Alexandria Bay."

The names of the businesses and details of the various buildings became well known to me as the months and years passed, but on that first visit I was impressed to see so many buildings from the end of nineteenth and the beginning of the twentieth centuries. Stone buildings of both granite and limestone were numerous even though wood was the predominant construction material. I was further surprised to see so many three story buildings with ornate cornices.

Within a few weeks I could make the same walk down Church Street and recognize each business by name particularly those businesses we patronized. First came Folino's Shoe Store on my right and Weller's Garage and Weller's Movie Theatre on the left. Next to the garage were the Chez Paris Restaurant, Henry's Market and the Corner Pharmacy. On the shoe store side of the street was the three-story Argonne Inn with both accommodations and a restaurant. Collins & Kellett Hardware was next to the Inn and Guerrieri's Men's Shop was on the corner across from the pharmacy where Church Street intersected James Street.

James Street is only four blocks in length, but businesses lined both sides of the street. Turning right and walking down James Street I passed many more businesses including Guerrieri's Women's Shop, Pearl's 5 & 10, a second hardware, the Homestead Restaurant, a couple of curio shops, and the colossal Crossman House Hotel that was torn down the next year.

At the end of the street was the Uncle Sam Tour Boat Line. A fleet of wooden tour boats, a large parking lot, and a public dock marked the north end of James Street. This area was known as the "Lower Bay."

"Is this the end of the town?" I asked.

"It was all I saw on my walk earlier," Betsy said.

On my first tour that morning with Deb and Betsy, we walked back from the Lower Bay along the opposite side of James Street to see the one block extension leading to the "Upper Town Dock." Next to the Corner Pharmacy was the St James Hotel, which had become a popular saloon rather than a place to stay. Betsy and I stopped briefly across the street from the St James waiting for Deb to catch up. I took the opportunity to look over the hotel, which had marble columns standing sentry at the entrance. The columns supported a substantial covered porch extending out toward James Street from the second floor. To the left of the hotel was the building that housed the Corner Pharmacy. It resembled many of the buildings I saw that morning. It was three stories of wood construction with the pharmacy on the ground floor. I took little notice of the rooms on the upper two floors, and I never did inquire or learn what function they served.

As we moved down the rest of the block toward the dock we passed a car dealership showroom then Vince Cavallario's Market and finally a curio shop belonging to Mike Cavallario.

Most all of the businesses we saw that day have become a footnote in the history of the Village. There have been an inordinate number of fires in the Alexandria Bay community particularly during difficult economic times. The Corner Pharmacy building, the St James, and the garage on the other side of the St James all burned in separate fires in the years that followed. Other buildings like the Argonne Inn and Weller's Garage have been transformed into new businesses. Weller's Garage became Cavallario's Steak House and the theatre was torn down to provide added parking space. The shoe store is now a boutique. The Upper Town Dock and the bay waterfront have resisted dramatic changes. The boats have evolved, but the dock itself looks very similar to that first time I saw it.

When Deb, Betsy, and I reached this main town dock, I stopped and said, "I'm going to need to take a few minutes here to check this out." The dock was at least the length of a football field and it curves to the right in keeping with the shape of the bay. The Paul Tour Boat Line, Van's Marina and Cranker's Machine Shop radiated into the bay from the right. Rogers Marina, Hill's Motor Court and Hutchinson's Marina guarded the shoreline on the left.

Looking into the distance beyond the dock I became aware of how many islands there are in this part of the 1000 Islands. Numerous islands appeared to be an easy row from here. What a contrast from our home in

Santa Barbara where the Pacific Ocean stretches toward the horizon with one of the five Channel Islands usually visible some twenty miles away.

I had boating experience living in Santa Barbara including going to sailing camp one summer. Sailing and deep-sea fishing were the two main boating activities on the Pacific coast. What I saw here was quite different. I had never seen such an array of wooden powerboats anywhere like the ones I saw here.

Deb was finally in her element because the town dock was clearly a place to stroll, and perhaps linger now or late at night for a few extra moments with a special sweetheart. There wasn't a sailboat in sight, and I learned why later. Several cruisers were tied up. I'd seen similar cruisers at the Santa Barbara Harbor, but the runabouts, the Paul and Pilgrim tour boats, and the 1000 Islands breed of fishing boat were all new to me.

Most all of the local boats were wooden hulled at that time. I remember a couple of fishing guides picking up customers at the dock. Their boats were generally a little more substantial in appearance. These boats had a wider beam and a more freeboard than the go-to-town boats I saw. Fishing-guide boats were almost all outfitted with some type of top. Some tops were constructed of wood and a permanent part of the boat while others were canvass. Fishing guides realized that rainy weather or choppy water could still be good fishing weather if their boat was suited for the conditions.

As I ambled further along the twelve-foot wide dock, I sensed that I was in the presence of a friendly community of boaters. I remember one couple sharing my appreciation of the setting as I walked by. They were drinking coffee on the back deck of their Matthews cruiser.

A generous number of wooden benches were stationed at convenient intervals for folks to sit and soak up the relaxing atmosphere. We didn't sit down, but I, in particular, took my time looking over an entirely foreign species of everyday conveyance.

After hundreds of visits to the town dock, I became familiar with the various manufacturer names and the individual boats. The tour boats were built by local concerns like Hutchinson Brothers, W.E. Adkins and the Ward family. I soon learned about the builders of cruisers like Matthews, Chris-Craft, and Richardson. Builders like Lyman and Hutchinson produced utility boats abundantly. Luxury speedboat manufacturers included Garwood, Century, Shepard, and Chris-Craft.

Windshields and varnished wood decks appeared to be standard equipment on just about every boat I saw that morning. Unlike the fishing-guide boats, most of the runabouts and speedboats had little freeboard. These boats were designed to ride close to the water and to skip over calm water or small waves.

One boat did not fit in. I saw Hydrodyne manufactured this boat. It was a shiny fiberglass craft, and I supposed it was designed for water skiing. Ironically, with the passage of years, fiberglass boats became the norm and the classy wooden boats became the rarity.

Deb checked her watch as we passed the Corner Pharmacy on our way back to the motel, and I recall her saying, "How's about stopping for breakfast at the Chez Paris? Mom and Dad won't be ready to go anywhere for another few hours."

I like a scenic view when dining out if it's an option. I remember that day and numerous others to follow because of the unique booth tables. The customer walked up several steps and through the front door into the dining area. The booth tables that I favored are positioned next to large plate glass windows that measure about six-feet square. Being less than six-feet tall, I found it is an odd sensation to sit on the very edge of the sidewalk and watch passersby from the vantage point of an eight-foot tall man.

The Chez Paris was a simple diner-style café that only served breakfast and lunch. This was a no frills restaurant with reasonable prices. Many customers ate there regularly judging from the way they interacted with one another. Trophy sized fish were mounted near the ceiling over many of the booths. Numerous photos of the proprietor, Frank Cavallario, and celebrities like professional boxer, Carmen Basilio hung lower down on the same walls. As we were preparing to leave we saw a sign that read, "Recommended by Frank Cavallario." We laughed in unison realizing that the owner was recommending his own business. Henceforth, the Chez Paris became known to our family as the "Cheese Paris." The restaurant is still in business as I detail this in 2013, and like the Upper Town Dock, the Chez Paris has survived essentially unchanged.

As the decades passed, the convenience of coming to the town dock, and doing all our shopping within walking distance of the boat, dwindled and eventually ended altogether as businesses moved to the outskirts of the village. The synergistic friendly relationship between village residents and islanders likewise became less congenial.

CHAPTER 7

❧

Mansions and the Shipping Channel

TYPICAL OF GOING anywhere with Dad, it was approaching one o'clock when the five of us assembled at Wilford's dock. *Buzz* rocked from side-to-side and was generally unsteady because of its narrow beam and primarily rounded bottom. It required some agility to move around in this craft or simply to get on board. Dad got aboard first and offered a hand to Mom, who sat in the narrow stern seat with Betsy. Dad got the motor running, and while he warmed up the engine, I tended the lines and cast us off. Deb, my dad, and I sat up front where Dad operated the boat. We all kidded about the decrepit condition of *Buzz*. Betsy said, "Any bets on whether this tub will make it to the island and back?"

Betsy and Mom continued to chat nervously while gesticulating and generally showing their excitement relative to the outing. Deb, Dad, and I had the benefit of a successful trial run in *Buzz* the previous evening which made us less wary of breaking down. Dad pointed out more landmarks, like the shop where Mancel Root worked, as we retraced the previous evening's route out of the Otter Creek channel by all the boathouses and cottages. With five passengers, *Buzz* was full to capacity.

Someone took a picture of us that afternoon and looking at it refreshed my memory of Mom in particular. She was wearing a bright raspberry colored dress and a beige, broad-brimmed straw hat with artificial flowers circling the base of the crown. Daisies, red roses and some species of blue flower made the ensemble complete. A decorative hat was Mom's trademark.

Hats and colorful dresses were a testament to her outgoing congenial personality. She is smiling and appears alert as she points at something on the opposite shore. Mom was open without malice. She had no hesitation about letting a person know what was on her mind. She particularly enjoyed entertaining and social occasions. Her enthusiasm and intelligence made her popular with those who shared her company.

Mom's hat collection

She favored straw hats, and she bought dozens that had some sort of ornamentation attached. She named her personal boat the *Mad Hatter.* She had been an accomplished tennis player growing up in Pasadena, California, and she continued to play as an adult. At five-feet tall, she was short in stature but wiry-strong with well-defined muscles in her arms and legs. Mom has a definite tan in this photo, which was typical. Deb and I are also tanned and apparently inherited our tanning ability from her. Dad and Betsy only burned, and they look like they seldom venture out into the sun. Aren't genetics interesting?

I watched carefully and took note of what steps Dad performed to operate a powerboat like the *Buzz.* I knew boating would become second nature as I gained experience, but sailing in the ocean hadn't provided me any practice for running or landing a twenty-four foot launch like this. My mind was working at warp speed to process so many new and unfamiliar experiences.

This trip of a little more than a mile began mid-day unlike the previous evening's tour in semi-darkness. We passed the Edgewood Resort and the Upper Town Dock. Perhaps because it was daylight and other boats were out on the River, Dad opted to take the main channel route rather than the inside channel we had taken the previous evening.

Having grown up in Santa Barbara, I was no stranger to grand estates, but what I saw here exceeded anything I had imagined. I knew this section of the River was known as Millionaire's Row, but everywhere I looked stood another mansion. As we neared the main channel we passed the foot of Cherry Island, and a four-story, forest-green mansion with a small section of attic above the third floor. The structure rested on a granite outcropping twenty or thirty feet higher than the level of the River. A large covered porch provided views of the main channel, the inside channel, town, and the town dock. A pair of turret-shaped second floor rooms was unlike anything I'd ever seen. The construction reminded me of a Popsicle with a pointed witch's hat on top, and a sticklike support stabilizing the structure from below. Two oversize stone chimneys were visible as they stretched above a complicated roofline that displayed peaks and dormers. I couldn't help but wonder how anyone would ever reroof such a menacing creation.

We rounded Cherry Island and headed up the main shipping channel toward Comfort. Without a pause, a second Cherry Island mansion greeted us. This mansion had a red roof and was another example of complicated rooflines and unique design. A four-sided square tower with a steeple roof rose from the center of the structure. It reminded me of a pioneer fort watchtower.

As we moved up the channel the next island bordering the channel is what was known then as Jewel Island. A flashing-green light is secured at the top of a twenty-foot steel pole at the upriver end of the island. The pole has been driven into the rock where it meets the water. I noted a similar marker on Cherry Island as we passed a third mansion at the head of that island. This is one of many channel markers that assist boaters and pilots as they make their way through the St Lawrence Seaway.

We took the inside route on the opposite side of the island from the main channel. We passed a large two-story boathouse with living quarters on the second level, but there was no house on this island. I asked Dad why there was no house. He explained that a St. Lawrence Seaway consortium widened the Seaway in 1958 and that half of Jewel Island including the stone mansion was dynamited. "What happened to all the debris?" I asked.

"The river is at least two hundred feet deep here and the debris simply sank to the bottom." Dad said.

The Seaway provides an important artery in transporting goods like iron ore, coal, grain, petroleum and other important commodities to North American markets both internally between Canadian and the United States as well as international markets including Africa, the Middle East and Europe. Ports like Chicago, Detroit, Duluth, Buffalo, Toronto, and Quebec all benefit from the commerce this waterway provides.

The width of the shipping channel varies. The River bends around a corner near Jewel Island. This section of the Seaway is known as the

"Narrows." Many years after my first trip up the main channel a "scratch" golfer visited Comfort Island. He attempted to drive a ball from Comfort Island across the channel to the not so distant shore but came up short. Had he been able to tee the ball at the edge of the shipping lane, I have no doubt that he would have easily reached land from that distance. A dozen times I have witnessed two freighters forced to pass in this narrow turn in the river, and I understand why specialized captains come aboard to pilot ships through this fifty-mile stretch of the river.

I felt the *Buzz* fishtailing with the increased current near Jewel Island. I looked over the gunwale as the water rushed by, and I saw whirlpools at the points where current and counter-currents intersected. I learned later that the counter-currents occur near the shoreline and are called "eddies."

Once past the Jewel Island boathouse, Comfort Island came into full view. A couple of hundred yards would bring me to the landing I'd anticipated for so long.

CHAPTER 8

— ✂ —

Let's Go Ashore for a Firsthand Look

EVEN THOUGH DAD had spent many summers at the island, he was at a loss where to land as we approached the shore. The beach that faced Jewel Island would have worked for a rowboat or a small outboard, but it was too shallow for an inboard with a shaft, strut, and rudder like *Buzz.* No landing spot was possible going west toward the main channel so Dad began idling east toward the New York main shore while looking for a suitable spot. The cement seawall next to the beach had jagged rocks protruding from the semi-collapsed wall, and like the beach, the water was too shallow.

I watched as Dad maneuvered further around the East side of the island. He had one hand on the floor-shifting lever and the other on the steering-stick apparatus. The way he bobbed his head in looking over the side while fumbling with the shifting lever convinced me that Dad was nervous and uncertain how to proceed. I noticed that the current was minimal here near the foot of the island, which was one less variable to worry about. I stood up to help scout obstacles in our path. Dad explored the possibility of landing where the two boathouses had been located. I pointed out rock-filled wooden structures called "cribs" in our path. These cribs had once been used to support the boathouses. Interspersed with the cribs were timbers that floated partly submerged. They had been left behind when the boathouses were demolished. To complete the gauntlet, lifting jacks used to raise boats for the winter peered up from the bottom menacingly where they had come to rest when the docks were removed. This was surely not a suitable place to land.

While Dad continued looking at the remnants of the boathouse structures, I spied another dilapidated structure further up the east shoreline, and I said, "Look Dad that old shack has a dock in front of it."

I wondered what sort of building this was. A cement dock was built next to the shed, and a curved lifting davit was built into the dock. Dad's frown turned to a smile that I translated as relief now that the landing problem had a clear solution. "What is this building?" I asked.

"It is the coal house that was used to store coal for the steam yachts, the Dockash stove, and the house furnace."

I stepped up to the dock from the boat gunwale and tied the lines to the round tying-rings that were anchored into the cement when the dock was built. The cement was beginning to flake and chip much like the rest of cement work that bordered the shoreline. Our engineer neighbor once told me that cement begins to return to its original state of sand and powder after eighty years, which explains what was happening to this dock at that time.

It was a little tricky getting out of the boat and up onto the dock that was two or three feet above the level of the boat. Mom already knew what to do. She sat on the dock first then swung her legs around and stood up. This maneuver works well getting into or out of a boat when the water is low or the dock is high.

Blueberry bushes, lilacs, shrubs and unkempt grass made me think of bushwhacking in the California backcountry. The path was totally overgrown with blueberry bushes that wrapped around my ankles causing me to trip more than once. Gnats circled me for a closer look and a few mosquitoes joined the parade with more serious intent. Overall the bugs were relatively tame. In visits to the New England woods and Adirondack trails near Lake Placid in the years that followed, I learned how lucky we were in the 1000 Islands as black flies and multiple platoons of mosquitoes did not thrive here like those that drove me back to the car before my hike had hardly begun in those other venues.

I stopped to look around when I reached the bend. Huge flagstones that measured five feet wide and three to six feet long had been seated in the ground one-after-another to produce this unique walk.

Deb was checking-out the areas adjacent to the walk that had obviously been landscaped decades ago. I came to have a look, and we exclaimed in unison, "Too much!" To our disbelief a bed of yellow lilies had continued to grow in a rock-bordered bed on the uphill side of the walk. We talked about how hearty some of these plants were that they could survive decades of total neglect.

A few of the lilac bushes were in the final stages of blossoming. I came to regard these bushes as a nuisance because their flowering period only lasts a week or two and the rest of the time they grow out of control. Nonetheless, I forgave the plant its shortcomings because I treasured the sweet smell they emit during their bloom.

I discovered a 1961 Polaroid shot taken from the spot where Deb and I stopped to take stock of the setting. The photo has faded significantly, but it helps me remember the sorrowful state of the house and grounds when we first returned. The grass is waist high and a bush has taken root under the house then climbed up the square lattice to become a fixture on the front porch seven feet above ground level. There are a dozen, twelve-foot wide steps leading up to the front porch and a railing on each side. The railing on the channel side is still in place while the railing on the left is lying on the ground.

The roof was mostly covered with cedar shakes at that time. I say "mostly" because I remember picking up a large number of these shakes that had rotted and fallen to the ground when I began the task of civilizing the lawn after it had been unattended for at least twenty-five years. The roof had bare spots in plain view as a consequence of no one being there to the address the need for new roofing. The old photo served to refresh my memory relative to other details like sections of metal flashing that had come loose and were lying askew on the upper roof where they served no useful purpose.

I had a sense of relief thinking that we had come to the rescue of Comfort Island in a nick of time as if scripted for a Hollywood movie. I'd seen abandoned buildings that eventually collapsed as a consequence of uninterrupted neglect. Barns no longer in use in poor rural farmlands came to my mind as prime examples with roofs caving in and in some cases the whole structure collapsing. Our grand old Victorian homestead seemed to be on course for a similar fate without intervention soon.

Deb and I forged ahead to get a look at the front porch. I was the first to get to the front steps. As I placed my weight on the first stair and was in the process of stepping toward the second, the stair collapsed beneath me. It threw me off balance and I heard my tennis shoes slap the sidewalk as I landed upright with a jarring skid. I was relieved I wasn't further up the steps where I could have taken a serious header. I tried the right side of the stairs where the railing was shaky but still attached. I tested each step before moving on to the next. I chuckled to myself as I imagined how scary it would be walking around on the roof, which appeared to be more rickety than the stairs.

The rest of the steps were still in reasonable condition, and within a few moments Deb and I stood on the hallowed porch. As someone who had recent experience building and enjoying crude tree forts, I admired the vantage point afforded me by this particular perch. Down through the years more than one guest has characterized this particular spot as a "commanding view." Looking northeast, I was able to see several miles of the main shipping channel downriver. The view west was a picture-window opportunity to watch ships making their way through the Narrows.

I looked to see what Mom, Betsy and Dad were doing. I smiled to see Mom dabbling her feet in the cool water at the beach. Soaking her feet had become something of a fetish for Mom. I remember occasions when she got Dad to stop by a roadside stream or other convenient body of water to "dabble." I conjectured she adopted this compulsion as an outlet for the stress associated with traveling with my vague and slow moving father. Dad, for his part, was walking off distances on the east shoreline where the boathouses had been. I was quite sure he was picturing where another boathouse might best be placed.

The front door had no lock so Deb and I stepped inside to see if we could find a couple of chairs for sitting on the porch while we waited for the rest of our contingent to reach the house. I immediately realized I was standing in the midst of a museum. The setting reminded me of some of my first remembrances associated with "Grandpoppy" and "Grandmommy" Lee's house when I was still in diapers. Mom's dad and mom lived near us in Pasadena before we moved a hundred miles north to Santa Barbara when I was six. Their house was old and had a similar musty smell.

I recall looking up with wonder at the ceiling that was twice as high as I was used to seeing. The walls had murals painted onto the plaster. Because several shutters, used to protect the windows from winter storms, had not been removed from this section of the house yet, it was quite dark inside, and I was not able to make out specific details of these wall embellishments. I did notice a number of Impressionist paintings depicting local River scenes dotting the walls as well. This was before Dad had electricity brought to the house and our side of the island. The simple task of flipping a switch to illuminate a dark room would have to wait another year at Comfort Island.

Deb and I spied a couple of wicker rocking chairs clustered in the corner of a living room that was overflowing with furniture. We headed the chairs to the porch. I was itching for Dad to provide us with a guided tour of the house, but I had waited fourteen years, and I supposed a few more minutes would be relatively painless.

What a foolish thought it was to think Dad would join the rest of the group in timely fashion. Mom and Betsy joined us after Mom let her feet dry, and got her shoes back on. I fetched two more chairs and the four of us waited for Dad together. Dad moved up to take a closer look at the coal house first, and the next thing we knew he was out on the downriver point adjacent to the main channel peering at something he seemed to find important there.

I could see Mom's agitation growing as she lit another cigarette and brushed her hair back with first one hand and then the other. She muttered something I couldn't quite hear, but by the way she pursed her lips, I figured she was ready to clobber him. She shouted for him to come join the rest of us. I lined-up a fifth chair just in case Dad made it before dark.

Dad took one more detour to verify that the pump house, which supplies water to the house and grounds, was still in its original location. To me, the pump house looked to be in the best condition of any of the buildings on the island I'd seen so far. The pump house is located down next to the main channel shoreline. This building has nearly as many Victorian flourishes as the house. The shape of the building is that of a windmill tower where the sides have been walled in. The base of the building is 14 feet on each side and that tapers to a smaller flat roof that is 4 feet on each side. The roof has a steep pitch and was covered with cedar shakes. The outside of the main building is covered with cedar shakes as well, but these siding shakes have been painted yellow and cut to display a teardrop-shaped curve at the bottom edge. Stained glass has been used for the windows, which produces a multicolored hue inside. The top of the roof section has a small railing attached to a set of intricate spindles of Victorian persuasion. It was no surprise that the original water system consisted of a windmill on top of the building that conveyed water up the hill to a gravity-feed tank on top of a tall, narrow building behind the house.

The four of us continued to wait while we reassured Dad that the pump house was in the same spot that numerous seventy-five year old photos recorded it.

Dad stopped at the bottom of the steps to survey the defunct first step, the flopped-over railing and the bush growing on the porch. He shook his head in a gesture we all understood. I remember him saying, "It looks like we need to make a few repairs before we invite the Queen to come visit."

Betsy responded saying, "Boy, ain't that the truth."

I glanced at Mom, who looked very stern and not a bit amused by the day's pilgrimage. Unfortunately Mom spent much of her married life being frustrated by Dad taking so long to get anywhere or to get anything done. I never knew her to drink during the day, but she sometimes made up for her daytime abstinence at night.

Dad mounted the steps and sat down with the rest of us. It was after four o'clock by this time. Mom suggested she'd like to use the bathroom, but Dad advised her that the water system wasn't working yet. I saw Mom's facial muscles tighten and her eyes narrowed with this development. The tenor of the excursion had suddenly become even more tense, and I had a sense of foreboding. The happy family outing had come to an end when Mom said, "I'd like to go back to the hotel now."

Deb, Betsy and I were familiar with the tension and hard feelings between our parents. Betsy clearly prefers to avoid controversy and arguing. I suspected then and now that her avoidance of hostility had its roots in the relationship between Mom and Dad. I was somewhat conflicted by scenes like these, but I was too excited by all the newness I was experiencing to let it affect me on this occasion.

CHAPTER 9

_____ ❧ _____

Will It Be Edgewood, Pine Tree or TI Club?

WE RETURNED TO the Maple Crest without incident. _Buzz_ ran more smoothly, which caused me to recall the theory that machinery doesn't function well when it is left sitting for long periods. Now that it had been run a few times, _Buzz_ was running better regardless of the reason. The gaiety and anticipation of going to Comfort Island for the first time was not the same for me on the ride back, but I was thankful there were no major blowups.

When we arrived at the motel, Dad suggested we have dinner at the Edgewood Resort. The spell of gloom was thus broken, and we returned to our respective rooms to prepare for a fancy meal out.

One of the features of an irregular shoreline is that in some cases, it is shorter to go by boat than to walk or take the car. From Buzz's parking spot it was a only short diagonal across Otter Creek to Edgewood's back dock, but to go by land it was a considerably longer walk or drive. The idea of taking the _Buzz_ was quickly voted down, and the idea of walking was excluded from the balloting. We drove the longer distance around.

The entrance to Edgewood followed a road to the motel complex that was at least a quarter-mile in length. Midway between the entrance and the central motel complex was another entrance to an attraction named "Adventure Town." The theme of the attraction was the old West. It was closed for the day, but a coal burning locomotive and a stagecoach could be seen from the car as we passed by. As we drove up to the main building, I noted a bank of rooms to the right and behind us. I learned that these rooms provided housing for the employees. Edgewood had a multitude of other outlying buildings with motel rooms in each. Conventional rows of motel units were interspersed with old Victorian cottages in the style of Comfort Island. These early cottages presented the guest with an entirely different setting and experience from the more traditional units.

We wove our way past the gift shop and the registration desk to the dining room, where we were seated at one of the window tables that I'd seen from Buzz on our way to and from Comfort. The view of the River was spectacular. A freighter was only a few hundred yards from where we sat. Clearly it was on its way to some port in the Great Lakes. The green mansion with the popsicle-like rooms I'd seen at the foot of Cherry Island was closer yet on our left, and further into the distance on the right was Boldt Castle. From the little I'd seen of the 1000 Islands region so far, I was flabbergasted. The islands, boats, mansions and now the Edgewood were like going to Disneyland or another marquee attraction without the crowds or an admission charge.

When our beverages arrived, Dad proposed a toast to our first landing as a family on Comfort Island. I glanced quickly at Mom thinking that was a bad choice of toasts, and sure enough she was rolling her eyes toward the ceiling. Nonetheless, the toast did serve to get a dialogue going on how the family would deal with our return to the 1000 Islands, in general, and Comfort Island, in particular, for the rest of the summer.

Dad suggested that once we got the rest of the house opened up with the shutters off and the water system working, it wouldn't be all that Spartan to stay at Comfort. He reiterated that this amounted to just a little fixing up.

Mom was not in any mood for idle fantasy. In fact I remember her saying something along the lines of, "Are you kidding me? You suggest a little fixing up, but here Comfort is with no electricity, the water system isn't working, the boathouses and docks are gone, and the roof leaks. Bats will most certainly come into the house at night. I'm not staying there until this place becomes a lot more hospitable. I'll start searching for a civilized place to stay tomorrow."

Mom had made her wishes known in no uncertain terms. As dinner progressed, each of us gave our opinion relative to which resort we favored. I made my pitch for the Edgewood. Not only was Edgewood close to town, but it was an action spot as well. They had a beach, a pool, boat rides, water skiing in addition to "Adventure Town" adjacent to the motel. I would find it quite easy to drop by there to indulge myself in some water skiing or maybe just hang out with a pretty girl now and then.

Deb had no particular preference relative to staying anywhere except Comfort Island. Dad favored Pine Tree Point and the Thousand Islands Club. I viewed his input as being biased by the sedate atmosphere that was more in tune with his desire to sleep-in without disturbance. Mom wanted a tour of each option before making up her mind.

Betsy was in her element when it came to where to stay and what to do. She was independently minded and relaxed about exploring places on her own. She would later work as a travel agent, an adventure-travel writer and, eventually, a photojournalist. She had already checked out the options in the area, and she was soon leading the discussion. I recall her saying, "Okay you guys, get this, there are three resorts in the Alexandria Bay area, and they each have their advantages. We are seeing Edgewood tonight, and we can see Pine Tree and the TI Club tomorrow."

She did go on to say that staying with Mom in a civilized setting was okay by her, and we willingly agreed that Deb, Dad and I would start our stay roughing it at Comfort Island as a threesome.

CHAPTER 10

Could Pine Tree Take the Prize?

WITH BETSY ACTING as tour director, we spent the next day checking out the other two resorts. She suggested we sample Pine Tree Point for lunch while we took stock of what else they had to offer. This idea made sense to me, since being up and going by lunch hour was tailored to Dad's preferred daily routine.

Lunch would be followed by a return to the Maple Crest prior to heading to the Thousand Islands Club to see what they had to offer in addition to dinner that evening.

Pine Tree Point was in the opposite direction from Edgewood and about twice as far from town. We followed the road northeast and downriver to a quiet and somewhat remote setting from my perspective. I saw a lot of senior citizens as we parked and walked to the main building. I saw none of the Edgewood atmosphere that appealed to my teenage generation. The main allure I saw at Pine Tree was a handsome central stone headquarters with a scenic patio fashioned of flagstones and shaded by overhanging pines. A spacious dining room featuring large windows offered a panorama of the shipping channel and a view of Boldt Castle that was as good or better than the view from Edgewood.

While we sat eating, I looked around at some of the other patrons. I remember one couple that came in after us. I was wondering if the man would make it to his seat okay, as he seemed to be very feeble. What I assumed was his somewhat younger wife took his arm to assist him after he stumbled and nearly fell. He wore a tie and coat while she wore a dark plaid sleeveless dress and lots of gold jewelry. Betsy recognized her dress as a creation of some notable fashion designer, but I forgot the designer's name before we finished lunch. I watched the couple with curiosity after I noticed they hardly said a word to one another. By the way she kept looking around at the other tables and primping her hair, I sensed that she was bored.

As a teenager, I was looking for high-energy settings not old folks dosing off in the midst of their meal. I saw no one in the restaurant my age or younger. Unlike Edgewood, even the servers were older adults.

Dad spotted Pine Tree's owner, Cap Thomson, as we were getting ready to leave. Dad said, "I've got to stop and say hello."

Dad told Cap who he was and his connection to Comfort Island. We all made Cap's acquaintance before Mom, Betsy and Deb excused themselves and went to explore the grounds and the gift shop. I was curious to hear what this local legend had to say and I listened with interest as Cap reminisced about the early generations of Clarks on the river. He was a contemporary of my grandfather and my great uncles. He mistook my father for Dad's father, "Howdy, Mancel let's see, you must be about seventy-five now?"

My dad answered, "Well I probably look seventy-five but actually I'm only fifty-three."

I didn't need any fancy math to realize that if Cap was eighty-five that would make Dad's father about the same age rather than seventy-five. I sensed that Cap might be getting a little vague with his advanced years. Meanwhile, Cap moved on to the next Clark story saying, "Did I ever tell you about the time I went to visit on Comfort Island and Mr. Clark offered me some of that new fangled ginger ale. Well I took a big gulp and it fizzed back up through my nose and I got to coughing and wheezing. Grandfather Clark nearly rolled on the floor he was laughing so hard."

I thought this was a very funny story, and I felt a sense of pride that this pillar of the community remembered my forefathers with humor and high regard after so many years had passed. Even though I heard the same stories many more times thereafter I admired what Cap had accomplished. As an industrious young man, he had rowed people around the river for a small fee to get ahead then eventually moved up to a motorized tour boat business that continued to flourish long after his death in 1967.

My favorite story he told was about how he talked my great grand-father into renting his dog for the summer more than once. I never did tire of that story because it demonstrated just how clever this fellow had been in making money. I remember he had a special table at Pine Tree where he ate each evening next to a staircase that led to a special events dining room downstairs. He always dressed the same in a suit of matching trousers and jacket with a white shirt but no tie. When eating, he'd tuck his napkin into the top of his shirt.

Deb, Betsy and Mom had time to check out the pool, the docking area out back, the gift shop and the Ping-Pong room by the time Dad and I concluded our conversation with Cap. Dad was always ready to stop and chat at length to a perfect stranger. Those long delays drove Mom and us three kids crazy, but on this particular occasion, I was glad to have had the experience of meeting Cap Thomson.

I fully agreed when Mom said, "I think this place is a little too stogy for my taste." We returned to Wilford's motel and "freshened up" as Mom liked to say before we headed to the TI Club.

CHAPTER 11

❦

Perhaps the TI Club Will
Be the Top Choice

THE THOUSAND ISLANDS Club is located on Wellesley Island and almost directly across the channel from Edgewood in a small bay protected by more islands. Like going to Edgewood from Wilford's dock, it is a short ride by boat, but a much longer drive by car. One must follow a road southwest four miles from town passing Comfort on the way to the International Bridge that crosses the St Lawrence River to Wellesley Island along a route that links the United States to Canada. Once the bridge to Wellesley Island has been crossed, we followed an island road that retraced our drive in a northeasterly direction to the TI Club. A toll must be paid for the bridge and the distance is about fives times farther than taking a boat.

Wellesley is approximately ten miles long and four miles wide at the head of the island where it is widest. The west side of the Narrows across from Comfort Island is shaped by the Wellesley Island shoreline. The TI Club is downriver from Comfort Island. Before the Great Depression the bay adjacent to this resort was one of the most affluent sections of the river. The TI Club was built as an annex for the Thousand Islands Yacht Club. The Yacht Club and the illustrious stone Pullman mansion, where President Grant came to visit in 1873, were torn down as a consequence of the Great Depression and unaffordable tax levies.

The TI Club had a self-contained setting with a Seth Raynor designed golf course, clay tennis courts, an expansive pool, a hair salon, a snack bar, a golf shop and a well stocked gift shop. Swimming, tennis and golf lessons were all available with resident pros on location daily. For a person who was seeking a sporting holiday this was the place.

The operation was being run by Treadway Inns that summer. They had a spacious room available in an annex called the Chalet with concierge amenities. Dad had a special affection for this location having been active in the Yacht Club during his youth. He persuaded Mom and Betsy to chose this option for their stay.

Harry and Mary Champaign were in charge of concierge services at the Chalet. They were of Swiss decent, and had lots of experience in the hospitality business and were fun to be around. They screened visitors, took messages, provided ice and other helpful services to the four apartments in the building. They owned a Great Dane named "Prince" who took Harry and/or Mary for walks several times a day.

The TI Club had a staff comprised mostly of college students who boarded at one of the many small outlying buildings surrounding the hotel and Chalet. These employee residences all had names like the Gate House, the Dairy House, the Golf House and a catch-all quarters over the kitchen known as the "Zoo." The dining room was large and the meals were elaborate. Each member of the dining staff had a designated function. There was a salad server, a rolls server, a dessert server and a server who took main course orders. Peter "Salad" became a household name as we became friends with various members of the staff.

Mrs. Smith, who was stern and at least 70-years old, ran the restaurant in a no nonsense fashion. She had no gift for gab except with Dad who gained her favor by discussing his attempts to keep the Dockash stove going long enough to heat water for a bath. Apparently she had experience with the same old stove as a young girl. The help referred to her as "Old Horseface."

CHAPTER 12

❧

Let the Exploring Begin

WITH MOM AND Betsy preparing to settle into the cozy Chalet, it was time for Dad, Deb, and me to do everything we could to make things as hospitable as possible at Comfort. Getting the plumbing going was everyone's top priority. A local plumber named Gerald Slate came and patched up rickety pipes while replacing the lead ones where it was conveniently possible. He helped me get the Briggs & Stratton gas-powered pump working long enough to pump some water into the pressure tank under the house.

My relationship with the Briggs & Stratton pump was troubled right from the start. Sitting idle for decades surely did nothing to make the motor run with ease or reliability. It routinely took lengthy sessions of repetitive cranking to eventually get it started. If I left it unattended, it often quit without notice and was twice as hard to start a second time. Occasionally I banged the gas tank with my fist in a fit of extreme frustration. This repeated pounding gradually gave the tank a unique shape. I must confess I used a lot of bad language. I thought perhaps that bad language was the key to starting stubborn devices.

I recall one particularly rough session where I eventually went to the house to take a break and have a snack. Dad was in the kitchen. When I began venting my frustration, Dad said, "You know that old wooden stool down there?"

"Yup. I sit on it on occasion."

"Comfort's original caretaker, George Root, had the job of starting that stubborn motor before you. He was in his mid-fifties by then. He'd sit on that stool and crank a while, and if it didn't start right away, he'd take out his pipe and relax a few minutes while having a smoke. After his smoke, he'd crank a little more. He always got it started. It could take a long while or a few seconds. It didn't matter to him."

I got the point, and Dad was right. At that time of my life, I was impatient and wanted everything done right now. Impatience was not an ingredient in the recipe for starting that motor.

Like everything else that never left the island when no longer needed or in use, there was one side of the pump house, which was like a cemetery for obsolete water pumping apparatus. A person could create an educational exhibit that tracks the advances in water pumping technology. The room is large enough that there is no sense of being crowded despite a jumbo-sized steam-pump connected to a flywheel with a two-foot diameter, several gearboxes, and a half-dozen other mechanisms that either didn't work or became obsolete. The Briggs & Stratton gas pump was simply the most recent addition to the Comfort Island waterworks. I've always thought it was ironic that the original pumping solution of a windmill was both trouble-free and required no fuel to operate. The resource of wind is abundant where the building was placed. How come no one saved a remnant of that artifact?

Dad said, "Make yourself at home" as he headed to *Buzz* to take the plumber back to town. I took him up on his suggestion entering the house through the front double-doors. The door on left side nearest the coalhouse dock has the doorknob and a brass doorknocker while the other door lacks such ornamentation and remains closed unless something large is moved into or out of the house. The stairway to the second floor is just to the right of the doorway.

Moving inside I launched a tour of the house beginning with the first floor. Now that the rest of the shutters had been removed I could get a clear look at the interior. It was apparent that things hadn't changed much since my great grandfather arrived in 1883. The old dark-brown sofa and stuffed chairs looked and smelled their age. The house was musty, which was no surprise since it hadn't been fully aired out in at least twenty-five years. The lighting in the living room was good thanks to four windows that measured four-and-a-half feet wide and nine feet tall.

I walked through the living room to the dining room. The first thing I noticed was that the dining room was darker than the living room. A quick check of where the light was coming from solved the mystery. The dining room had half as many windows as most of the other rooms.

A Japanese paper parasol with a diameter of seven feet hung over the dining table. Wooden decorative shelves were affixed to three of the four walls in the dining room with Japanese prints set in openings, and various other objects ranging from a stuffed loon to kerosene lamp shades were displayed on the flat surfaces. At night candles were lit and placed behind the prints to give them illumination. Just below ceiling level of the wall leading back to the living room is another mural depicting a formation of ducks in flight.

In the right-hand corner of the dining room, I opened the door and walked into the master bedroom. I only peeked into the paneled bathroom that was attached, but I did take note of the painted window shades and lace curtains in the bedroom. I could see the main channel out of the windows across from the doorway. I got my first view of our neighbor's grand house out the window next to the bed.

It took me several days to explore and become familiar with the myriad of rooms and passageways. The kitchen was my most common destination and I remember seeing it next. The side of the dining room across from the bedroom door funneled through a butler's pantry into the kitchen. A large coal-burning Dockash stove was on the opposite side of the room from the doorway. Next to the stove was a hot water heater with pipes running to the stove. On the wall to the right was a six-door icebox. A sink ran along the wall adjacent to the doorway where I was standing.

The specifics of various other rooms and cubbies gradually became well known to me, but during those first days, I was dealing with a sensory overload.

∽

CHAPTER 13

⸙

Alson S. Clark Left an Indelible Mark at Comfort Island

AS Clark painting of Comfort Island

MY GREAT UNCLE, Alson Skinner Clark, was born in 1876, and he arrived with the first wave of Clarks in 1883. He entered the "professional" art market by the age of nine. He had an uncommon ability to produce drawings for the freehand art class, and his fellow students who were in need of his services were willing to meet his price of fifty cents per drawing. This is a vote for those who believe that some gifted individuals are destined to follow a path for which they have a flare and talent.

Most of his paintings are either oil on canvas or oil on board. He traveled and painted extensively in Europe and also did a series of paintings documenting the building of the Panama Canal. In some cases he took his easel and paints right into the canal excavation sites to capture the subject he had in mind. His later works included scenes from Mexico and California where he was a noted member of the California Plein-Air movement.

I have favored Impressionist painting for as long as I can remember, and I consider it no coincidence that I grew up surrounded by artwork expertly produced in this style. I like the fact that it is not an exact representation of the subject, but rather an interpretation of the subject by the artist. I find that I gain my greatest appreciation of such a work when I back up a few steps.

He was responsible for all of the murals and most of the artwork found throughout the house. Murals over the downstairs fireplace and in the dining room added to the sense I had on my first visit of walking into a museum. The Oriental theme became popular with many artists following Commodore Matthew Perry's visit to Japan in 1853-1854. Comfort Island was strongly influenced by this theme, including grass matting that can still be found on some sections of floor. In 1961, most of the floor was covered with this material.

ASC painting looking toward main channel

Many of his paintings on the first floor were stunning. Hundreds of times I walked in the front door to be greeted by a painting of two trees by the river. The painting hangs over the piano, and without taking into account the frame it is more than three feet high and four feet wide. A full-grown pine tree stands a few feet apart from a maple of slightly shorter stature as they embrace with intertwined limbs. Several red maple leaves suggest fall is on the way. The foreground is dominated by the gray granite outcropping and wisps of summer grasses now turning reddish brown. Beyond the trees is the river with a range of blues, greens and browns that offer reflections of the immediate shoreline and the palisades and bluffs seen in the distance across the river. The weaving of the bright colors with short, well-placed palate strokes and a multitude of colors says much about why I favor the impressionist genre more than any other.

I continued my tour moving upstairs. As I began ascending the stairway at the channel side of the living room, I looked out the shorter window on my right at the pump house and the main channel. When I reached the landing two-thirds of the way to the second floor hallway, I glanced through a second window with a treetop view of the channel and yard, but I found the view out the window to be secondary to murals of Japanese geishas that accompanied me, as I turned left up the shorter flight of stairs. I remember being unable to contain an audible, "Wow!" as I reached the top of the stairs. On the wall in front of me, I came face to face with two more geishas that had been painted bigger than life.

As I walked down the hall, I counted five spacious bedrooms and a bathroom across from the fifth bedroom that faced the Papworth's. Surrounding the bathroom entrance is another exquisite mural depicting a fortified Germanic township with a moat. Stonewalls enclose the village and a conspicuous clock tower sits above a gate located where a bridge crosses the water-filled trench. A few peasants make the mural complete as they go about their daily business. A banner at the top of the mural encapsulates the title of "Alt Nemoberg." This mural is like others that have begun to flake a little more with each passing decade. We have done some research about ways to preserve this artwork, but the methods are quite expensive. It's hard for me to guess if the artwork or even the house will survive for future generations to enjoy.

ASC mural in upstairs hallway

I noticed on my way back to the stairway that one of his Japanese murals in the hallway was dated "Oct 25 '08." After staying late in the fall myself a few times, I chuckle knowing that the weather can be very forbidding anytime after Labor Day. I have imagined Alson and perhaps some painter friends getting cabin fever and taking to painting following several days of cold, rain and the north wind that takes direct aim at the front porch that time of year.

CHAPTER 14

∞

Where Are the Light Switches?

THE TASK BEFORE Dad, Deb, and I was to gather the essentials necessary to scratch out an acceptable existence in this hostile Comfort Island environment. One more night as a family at the Maple Crest and then we'd move to our respective residences. I realized, as did Dad and Deb, that we had important preparations to make. We needed to get kerosene for the oil lamps, gas for the water pump and ice for the icebox. The prospect of using the coal stove anytime soon was not a serious concern.

Dad had made a list and after he returned from taking the plumber back to shore, we scouted around to see what we had and what we still needed. We conducted our search together. In the storage room beyond the kitchen I spotted two tongs that resembled a giant pair of scissors with circular hand grips and two curved hinged pieces with pointed barbs at the lower end of each steel shaft. "What are these for, Dad?"

"Those are ice tongs, Tad, and we're going to need those to fetch ice for the ice box."

Dad was making important discoveries of his own. Tucked into a drawer in one corner were wicks for the kerosene lamps. A couple of old miner's lamps were sitting under a table as well.

In a rare display of exuberance and vitality, Dad was up and ready to go by mid-morning of the following day. The plan was for Mom and Betsy to take the car and their luggage to the TI Club and to get settled in there. In the meantime, Dad, Deb, and I would get supplies, then proceed to Comfort where we'd get settled in too. Our clothes were already at the island after I loaded them into the Buzz the previous day and then hiked them up to the house while Dad and Gerald Slate got started solving the water pump and plumbing problems.

"See you tonight at seven." Dad said as Mom and Betsy headed the station wagon back down Crossman Street for the drive to the TI Club.

It was only a few blocks from Wilford's dock to downtown, but we now had no car to transport our supplies back to *Buzz*, and it was raining for the second straight day. Furthermore, the bow navigation light wasn't working on *Buzz*. We would now be using the boat after dark, and a lack of either the bow or stern running-light was dangerous and illegal.

The hand-operated bilge pump had become as important to the operation of the *Buzz* as the gearshift or the tiller. The wood bottom was in worse shape than the motor. I put on a rain slicker and walked over to the dock early to pump the water out so we could get going sooner rather than later. It routinely took me fifteen minutes each morning to complete the task. Dad and Deb arrived at the dock just before I finished pumping. Dad warmed up the engine then he piloted the boat to Rogers Marina, which was around the corner from Otter Creek and Wilford's on our right as we entered the upper bay. The gas dock was crowded when we arrived. We left the boat on a side dock so they could fix the light when they had a lull.

"Let's go to the Cheese Paris for brunch so we can eat and get out of this rain." Deb said. Dad lobbied for the Homestead Restaurant where he could have an adult beverage with lunch, but he acquiesced realizing that this was a workday and there wasn't time to dawdle over a meal. When we finished eating, Dad and I walked across the street to Collins & Kellett Hardware while Deb took sandwich orders for the three of us, and she proceeded to Cavallario's Market & Deli to have our sandwiches made. Deb also picked up cereal, milk and orange juice as survival rations for the next morning. At the hardware, Dad purchased a gas can and a dispenser for kerosene, which they filled there. I carried the two cans as we walked back to Rogers.

Rogers had been in business for a long time and Dad remembered doing business there before his father died in 1928. Ray Sr. and his two sons, Ray Jr. and David, ran the operation as a team in 1961. Ray Sr. must have been nearly seventy or perhaps older when I met him that day. He was a bear of a man with sparse gray hair. Junior, as his eldest son was called, likewise had a big frame and wore glasses. David was of similar height, but he was trim compared to his dad and brother. Like his dad, David was going bald. David had an impetuous bent that found an outlet in his taste for high-performance boating whereas Junior was more inclined to cruise the river at a pedestrian speed in a more substantial vessel.

A corrugated metal building was closest to the parking area and downtown. The building covered two slips. Each slip was about fifty-feet long and twelve feet wide. A sizable work area was an integral part of the structure with a cement floor extending onto dry land from where the slips ended. Boats could be hoisted from the water into the work area for extensive woodworking or other major repairs. Another building was next to the first with only a narrow walkway in between. This building was constructed with wood, and it contained a machine shop and the front office through a side door.

The machine shop was teeming with old motors, gear assemblies and other mechanical accessories lined up like troops in revue. It didn't take me long to learn that this was Ray Sr.'s personal treasure chest. The senior member of the trio was a master at devising strategies to repair a customer's broken machinery with spare parts he had collected here. I remember there being just enough room for a narrow path to the doors and workbench. The cement was stained with grease and oil beyond cleaning. The enclosure had a rank odor of gasoline and oil residue.

We did a lot of business at Rogers that year and in the years to come. Their expert woodworker Willy Plimpton replaced the *Buzz's* bottom in 1966. Our mission on this day was to replace the light, get gas for the boat and water pump, and ice for the icebox.

I know the date because after carrying the ice and kerosene to the house, Dad brought out the guest book saying, "Sign-in, Son, and become an official part of the island history." I made my initial entry that rainy afternoon, and it reads, "June 21, 1961 (Tad Clark) Mancel T. Clark III, First trip to East and Island. Lots of Rain but still impressive. Intend to spend several months here. Will try to restore house and grounds if possible?" Not many more naive comments have ever been written in the Comfort Island guest books than my reference to restoring the house and grounds as though I'd have it done in a week or two.

It was still raining and foggy, which was a good excuse to thumb unhurriedly through the guest book pages in awe of the exquisite penmanship I was seeing. I knew about quill pens and I'd seen photographed examples, but like viewing a Van Gogh picture in a book and then seeing the actual painting, I understood that there is no comparison. I leafed through numerous pages not to read each comment but to indulge my fascination with the manner in which the letters and words had been formed.

After I'd had my fill of pretty shapes, I flipped back to the first page of the red leather-bound log, and there on the opening page was my great grandfather's first entry. "June 28th, 1883. Family and goods landed. Come to stay for the summer." Eight names in list form followed, beginning with my great grandparents, then my grandfather and great uncles before ending with the staff: Alson E. Clark, Sarah S. Clark, Mancel T. Clark, Alson S. Clark, Edwin H. Clark, Lena Johnson (cook). Maria Morton (maid), and Edward Field (butler) were listed in that order.

I reflected on how times had changed. In the days when my great grandparents spent their summers on Comfort Island, there were no modern conveniences. On a property this big and demanding, servants were needed to help perform everyday tasks that had been mechanized by 1961. The predicament for Dad, Deb, and me that summer was that the transition to modern conveniences had not yet begun. We were living in a 1880s world and ill prepared to perform the tasks of a legion of servants.

I had a primordial sense of uneasiness like I was isolated and some-how defenseless in my environment. The water pressure was flagging. I headed to the pump house to address running the pump long enough to get us through the night.

Dad, for his part, was focused on getting some of the kerosene lamps operating. The lamps and wicks hadn't been used for decades and a few wicks crumbled in his hands and had to be replaced altogether. Other wicks were okay and only needed trimming. Most of the lamps were de-signed for indoor use. A few fit into brackets suspended from a conve-nient post or panel while others were strictly table lamps. Our discovery of the mining lamps that would function in windy or rainy conditions would be a welcome convenience going forward. During our pioneering summer when we ventured out to dinner or to attend a social event, we placed one of these mining lanterns on the edge of the dock to assist our return after dark. The lantern not only showed us where to land, but it also made it easier to find our way through the underbrush to the main walkway that led to the house.

CHAPTER 15

᪥

Where Will We Sleep in this Big Old House?

WHILE SITTING ON the porch after I'd finished exploring the guest book, I recall Deb and Dad joining me to discuss what bedrooms we'd be using. I took a brief survey of the possibilities in my mind. The maid's quarters had three bedrooms, the upstairs proper had five bedrooms, and downstairs there was the master bedroom and a room next to it with a bed. The only problem I saw with where to sleep was having too many choices. With three of us in residence, the downstairs option would only accommodate two and no one was interested in being marooned in some distant corner of what some locals thought was a haunted house. The rooms in the maid's quarters had more serious weather damage than in the rest of the house, and they were small and had low ceilings. I soon realized that the bedrooms off the main second floor hallway were the obvious choice. The three of us headed upstairs to inspect the rooms firsthand.

In his youth, Dad had stayed in the bedroom under the tower. I noticed that the room was smaller than the other four rooms in this wing, but it did have two superior views. One window faced the Narrows and the second made it possible to see downriver where the ships entered the Narrows. The bed was tucked into the corner right next to both windows, which would allow me to zoom in on the boating traffic late at night. I remember Dad saying, "I always liked sleeping there. The ship lights reflecting off the water had a magical quality that made me imagine traveling to far away enchanted places."

I decided to give the room a trial run. Like Dad, I developed a special affection for this cozy nook that lent itself to an intimate view of freighters sliding by to the beat of powerful engines thumping their way up or down the channel. I was in awe of the vigilant pilots who were able to negotiate this precarious section of the river in darkness. A few flashing red and green markers outlined the route, but there is a sharp bend at the Narrows; the prospect of meeting an oncoming ship at this turn in darkness was not a job I considered inviting.

Deb chose the channel side room with the paint that took fifty years to dry. Dad explained, "Apparently when this room was repainted around 1920, motor oil was substituted for linseed oil." Each of us pressed our thumb into the bright yellow doorjamb to sample the surface that was still sticky. The flawed formula produced a paint that did not dry thoroughly during the forty-year interim.

I was no longer surprised to see that Alson Clark had left his artistic touch in this room too. Baskets of painted flowers decorated the open spaces toward the top of the eleven-and-a-half-foot walls. The ventilation window above the door leading to the hallway had flowers painted onto the center of the glass in shades of light blue and pink, and the window above the door to the adjoining bedroom was decorated with a smaller basket of flowers similar to the murals painted on the walls.

The room was larger than the tower room and the windows faced the same directions. The only drawback I noticed was the bed was located five feet or more from the optimal view. A door to the next room created a corridor that passed the channel side view. Furthermore, the windows facing the Narrows needed unoccupied space in front of them to access a small outside porch.

Dad knew which room he'd be taking before he left California. He, and Mom too when she moved in, would stay in the bedroom at the head of the stairs. It is a spacious room with a fireplace in the right hand corner. Two large windows look out at Keewaydin, which is a property across the back channel on the New York main shore. I took a close-up look out the window next to the fireplace, and I could see the coalhouse dock with the *Buzz* tied up there.

Two more windows were to my left as I entered the room. These windows looked down the main shipping channel. The windows pushed up into a slot in the ceiling to function as a door to a covered outdoor porch. I walked onto the porch to have a look. I remember thinking to myself, what a view. I gazed miles down the shipping channel where it began to recede into the background. Looking a little more to my right my eyes followed the route Dad, Deb, and I had followed on our first tour from the Maple Crest. I could make out the upper town dock, Rogers Marina and a few of the buildings at that end of Alexandria Bay. I felt like a bird perched in a tree as I looked down at the beach and the front lawn.

Like the dining room, a smaller but similar five-foot parasol was suspended over two single beds with a wooden table, also varnished, in between. A closet to the right of the entrance and another to the right of the doors leading to the covered porch completed the tour of this room.

Deb had the assignment of putting sheets on the beds for the three of us. Dad told her where the linen trunk was located, but like the kerosene lamps and other items, the linens had mostly been stolen. We each spent the first night with a sheet covering a horsehair mattress combined with a comforter playing the role of a top sheet. Had we been a family of outdoor camping enthusiasts, we would have been better prepared. Hiking and camping-out was not a popular activity when my parents were growing up, and neither of them ever developed a taste for roughing it.

CHAPTER 16

❦

Going Out to Eat Is Not as Simple as It Sounds

I REMEMBER THE first night of many dining out after we moved to Comfort. I exchanged my blue jeans for a pair of slacks and a dress shirt, and presto I was suited up for dinner. Dad, Deb and I assisted one another into the Buzz from the elevated coal dock. Thankfully the rain had ceased as Dad headed the boat down the main channel to the Thousand Islands Club where Mom and Betsy were now settling in. We turned left when we were opposite the end of the Cherry Island and the mansions there. Had we gone right instead, we would have passed the mansions and arrived at the Edgewood. Going left we dodged between rocks and islands as we approached the TI Club landing area. I recalled our previous visit when we came over the International Bridge by car looking for a place for Mom to stay.

The docking area was one of a kind. Two one-hundred-fifty-foot-long cement docks eighteen-feet apart provided the foundation for the covered boat-parking area. There were approximately twenty-five sturdy cement supports on each dock radiating up to support the roof. I thought it was odd that there were no walls for the docking area below.

A large room about forty-feet long rested on the supports at the entrance to the slip. Dozens of small-paned windows line each side of the building while other flourishes suggest a Victorian architectural slant. The hotel staff showed movies in the room overhead twice a week. I remember attending several features there that summer although, with the exception of the Hitchcock thriller *North by Northwest*, I've forgotten which ones.

The dining room was cavernous with several dining areas and alcoves all interconnected. Windows looked out at the pool and islands beyond. The main channel was farther away than at Pine Tree and intervening islands blocked some of the view unlike Edgewood. Otherwise the setting was tranquil with protection from the islands and shoreline. The water was consistently calm in this secluded bay.

I was used to eating out often with the rest of the family, and I would squirm and plot ways to take a break when the service was slow, or some member of the group wanted to linger after the meal. But with the immense Treadway Inn staff, the action was essentially nonstop. A bus person was at the table pouring water before the hostess left. A server was waiting to take drink orders. The roll-girl was on the heels of the server. After a short pause, our server returned and took our dinner order. I was glad to see Peter, the salad-man, when it was his turn to serve that course. We had met him on our first visit, and he knew about Comfort Island, and welcomed us "home" as he put it. We had fun joking with him on many occasions, and he became known to us as "Peter Salad." The roll-girl returned, the main course came and the empty plates were soon cleared away to make room for the dessert server. And so the meal would proceed.

Mom and Betsy walked to the dock with us to say, "Good night." The landing area was midway between the main building that included the dining room, and the Chalet where Mom and Betsy were staying. I remember giving Mom a hug, and Dad added a kiss to his hug. Dad promised that we'd meet at the same time the next evening to share another dinner together. Mom and Betsy went on their way while Dad warmed up the motor, and I cast off the lines.

The longest days of the year were upon us. We headed back to Comfort before dark on this occasion, but I remember later in the summer when we made the trip in darkness. I gradually learned to run the Buzz during the course of the summer. I recall asking Dad if I could run the boat home in the dark one night. I had no problem getting around that part of the river during the day, but I found it an intimidating journey in the dark trying to remember where shoals, rocks and islands were and how much room I needed to clear them by. I remember being greatly relieved to see the coalhouse dock that was being illuminated by the kerosene lantern Dad had placed at the end of the cement landing area. Once we landed safely, the ritual was always the same tying up Buzz. I would make sure the lines were tensioned properly so the fenders hanging from the gunwales protected the side of the boat from the rocking motion against the cement dock. I cleared much of the underbrush from the path leading to the main walkway to the house, which simplified the trek after dark.

CHAPTER 17

Getting Acquainted With Island Inhabitants

EACH NIGHT DAD left a kerosene lamp attached to a wall bracket going in the hallway in case any of us needed to use the bathroom before morning. I remember being relieved to have no unwelcome bat visitors that first night. The bats had set up a high-density housing project in the attic during the decades when they had the place to themselves. I went to take a look at the attic after I woke up the next morning. A narrow staircase continued up from the point where the stairs to the second floor ended. There were about twenty stairs and two landings on the way to the attic door. I pushed the door open at the top. I say, "pushed" with good reason because the attic floor was more than ankle deep with bat droppings. Dad had said, "The proper name for this excrement is guano, and it has value as a powerful fertilizer." As I recalled his words, I remember thinking we had a renewable resource and a potential moneymaker here.

On this first visit, I only took a quick look around at the interior. The ceilings were bare rafters some fifteen feet above the floor. There were several large rooms that had no walls intervening. Five dormers with dozens of interconnecting mini-windows provided ample light to the enclosure, but not enough to make out actual shapes of the bats tucked around the rafters. The atmosphere was stuffy, and a rank odor was overpowering. I could hear a chorus of bats squeaking high up in the eaves as they slept during the daylight hours. I had seen enough for one day, and I pulled the door shut as I returned to the front porch and the relief of fresh air. I returned to the attic to battle the bats before the end of the summer with the grandson of our neighbors, the Papworths. Deb, Betsy and I also explored the attic after the floor was cleared and the bats had taken up new quarters.

Later that morning I remember Deb and I followed Dad down the stone walkway by the pump house across a short flat and then up a few steps and to an adjoining stone path to the Papworth house. I was no longer surprised to see another three-story mansion. I felt the wind coming at me as we approached the house, and I soon learned that this southwest wind was the prevailing wind on the river. Mary and Ed Papworth were sitting on a glassed-in porch when we arrived. I intuitively realized that a screened porch would have been right in line with what was a ten-to-twenty mile-per-hour wind on this occasion.

The porch was an add-on, which was obvious after comparing the painted shake siding on the exterior of the house and seeing that it matched the shakes on the wall facing the porch. I wondered if it might have been an open porch at one time. The ceiling added credibility to my suspicion since it was painted a powder blue, which according to Southern lore keeps spiders and wasps away from open porches by fooling these insects into thinking the ceiling is actually the sky. The windows surrounding the enclosure were not fancy and measured approximately eighteen inches on each side. I learned quickly that Mr. Papworth placed practicality above style and beauty.

I think the senior Papworths were around sixty-five years old at that time. Ed was another big bear of a man built somewhat like Ray Rogers Sr. Ed and Ray were both oversized at the waistline but their legs seemed suited to a big but thinner man. Mary was robust but trim in comparison to Ed. All my memories of Mary or "Mrs. Pappy" as we came to know her were of a congenial and cheerful lady. She was overflowing with hospitality and good humor in contrast to Ed's gruff manner.

In her typical manner, she said something like, "How in the Sam Hill are you managing to survive over there? You two come right over anytime you need something."

As for Ed, his remarks were more along the lines of, "You got a lot of work to tackle in that rundown structure, Mancel. I'll come by in a day or two and give you my advice on how to go about working on it."

I recall Mrs. Pappy inviting Deb and I to the kitchen for a lemonade while Mr. Papworth and Dad continued their serious-sounding discussion. She informed Deb and me that six of her grandchildren would be arriving in less than a week, and she said, "I'll make sure they come over and introduce themselves." This was unexpected good news. Where we lived in Santa Barbara, we had few neighbors, and no other kids to pal around with in our immediate vicinity.

CHAPTER 18

⚬

I Need Wheels of My Own

I WOULD GENERALLY be up and ready to go at or before eight o'clock. I felt like I was wasting the day if I got up late. This was clearly the opposite of Dad most of the time and Mom on occasion. Being with Dad meant Deb and I had to entertain ourselves until Dad was ready to go out for errands or supplies around lunchtime. I had a use for some of those early hours, and my routine was well established that summer. I'd head to the coalhouse dock to pump out *Buzz,* which showed no signs of soaking up. Indeed, the leaks only got worse as the summer progressed. Once I got the bilge pumped, I'd cross to the other side of the island, and follow the walkway down the steep granite outcropping to the pump house. I learned to regard twenty minutes of hand-pumping the *Buzz* as the easier task compared to starting the infernal water pump.

A few days after we moved in, I recall poking around with Deb one morning after I'd finished my chores. We were checking out the area under the house. There was one small room next to the entrance under the front porch that had stone walls and a cement floor. It reminded me of a root cellar, but most of the floor surface was simply dirt. The whole area under the house was poorly illuminated, and I had to wait for my eyes to adjust before I could make out much of anything. I stumbled over the base of a rusty old coal furnace that was still in place but not serviceable, as we learned later. A little farther back I spied what appeared to be a long narrow rowboat that was pointed at both ends.

I'd read an account of the French penal colony named Devil's Island off South America, and for some reason a claustrophobic image of being

73

held captive flashed through my mind as I considered the prospect of having a method to reach shore on my own.

Deb and I celebrated like we'd found water just before collapsing in the middle of a sweltering desert. Deb said, "See if you can pull it out. Is there a rope on it? I'll help."

I replied, "What's this thing made of? It's heavy as lead."

We got Dad to help before we went to town that day, and the three of us dragged it out onto the front lawn. Carrying it was out of the question. A name was affixed to the bow with individual brass letters that read *Bobby*. Dad explained, "This was the family's St Lawrence Skiff that dated back to 1900."

I could see grass through the bottom, which was not a promising development. Dad said we'd look for supplies in town to get the bottom sealed up enough to use her again.

When we arrived in town, Dad reminded Deb and I that he had been a good sport about eating at the Chez Paris on the last trip, and now it was his turn to pick the Homestead, since we had no pressing need to get back to Comfort early. And so it was that Dad savored a noontime cocktail with his lunch.

The Homestead structure was one of numerous old limestone buildings in the region. I remembered passing the building on my first morning stroll through town with Deb and Betsy. After we entered, I noted a very odd arrangement. A passageway to the restaurant next door named the Spot was connected to this pristine old building. The Spot was a "greasy spoon" in the same category as the no-name diner that Dad and I had visited in Ames, Iowa coming East. That diner was where Dad had hopelessly miscalculated by taking on the Ol' Bessie Gristle Challenge.

The Spot and Homestead shared the same kitchen, and unfortunately for the customers, the same food. There were a number of tables with white tablecloths, but the ambiance ended there. The lighting was ultra-bright and the absence of interesting pictures or other wall trappings added to a cafeteria feel rather than a fine dining atmosphere. I stuck with my proven formula for such dives by ordering a sandwich that was pretty much foolproof. Peanut butter & jelly or ham & cheese were generally safe, and I ordered one or the other of these often.

After lunch we proceeded to Collins & Kellett to purchase supplies to reseal *Bobby's* bottom. As I recall, it was necessary to climb a few steps in order to enter the store where a long counter with a cash register extended toward the back end of the building. On the left were wooden shelves displaying hardware products of all descriptions. Behind the counter was an assortment of cubbies with other products. Nails, pipefittings and other necessities were down a set if wooden stairs in a basement area. I recall the wide wooden floorboards that had become recessed and misshapen from age and decades of heavy foot traffic. The floor was not painted and it took on the appearance of a rough-hewn floor in a frontier dwelling.

We assembled the tools and supplies we'd need, and I watched Dad as he indulged in one of his favorite pastimes of opening a new charge account. I felt sympathy for the store accounting staff because I knew of Dad's unique way of paying bills. In my visits to his office back in Santa Barbara, where I first saw the photo of Comfort Island and the steam yacht blowing the steam whistle, Dad would sit for hours with his bills and bill ledger.

I learned by observation and because Dad talked about it at home that he and Mom were experts at living slightly beyond their means. As income became available to pay some of the bills, Dad would calculate just how much of each bill he was prepared to pay. I recall sitting and watching him as he'd figure he could pay this much of this bill, and he'd write a check for that much and jot the amount down in his ledger. Then he would move down to the next bill due and repeat the process until the funds were exhausted.

Most of those who extended Dad credit were glad to get something, but I remember more than one creditor that became angry that the whole bill hadn't been paid. That was a different day and age. Now credit cards, penalties, and minimum payments accomplish the same thing. The difference is that the merchant gets paid right away, and the credit card company takes on the risk while benefiting from collecting interest charges that weren't added on to merchant bills in 1961.

I toted the Red-Lead bottom paint, the seam caulk, scrappers, sandpaper and putty knives to the boat. Dad and Deb stopped at Cavallario's Market next to the dock for a few groceries, and I picked up ice at Rogers before we returned to the island.

I'd seen a couple of sawhorses under the back end of the house, and I brought them around to the front lawn where the *Bobby* was resting on its side. Dad and I turned Bobby upside down. Deb held the hull steady as Dad and I hoisted one end of the skiff onto the first sawhorse. Deb moved the second sawhorse into place so that Dad, Deb and I could lift the other end into place. We then had Bobby in good position to work on the bottom in our efforts to make her watertight again. Deb was using a scrub brush to clean the crud off the wooden surfaces while I had a paint scraper that was taking off a good bit of the loose varnish.

I spun around to face the source of the voice that startled me. A boy about my age introduced himself. "Hello, I'm Hughie."

We exchanged introductions, and he told us that he was the eldest child in a family that included six kids. He explained that he had three brothers and two sisters. They had gotten to the island from their home in Syracuse shortly before he'd come over. Mrs. Pappy had sent him over to get acquainted, which I somehow knew without him telling me. I'd seen Syracuse on roadside signs and travel brochures, and I placed it one hundred miles south of the 1000 Islands. I learned it was the closest U.S. city of any real size.

Hughie only stayed a couple of minutes before saying he needed to get back to the house. He encouraged me to come over and meet his brothers and sisters in the morning.

I said, "I'll be over as soon as I finish my morning chores."

"Good deal. We'll probably be playing baseball on the flat."

I liked Hughie right from the start. We became close friends spending a lot of time doing things together that summer and the next summer too.

Deb and I continued to work on the bottom after Hughie left. I lightly sanded the spaces between the planks to make the surface receptive to the putty we were going to apply. The putty reminded me of peanut butter that had dried out a little too much, but as I pressed it into the narrow canals, it seemed to be sticking okay. I recollect Dad coming to inspect our work about the time we had finished puttying the major openings. He pointed out a spot or two we missed, but otherwise he gave us his approval. The putty would need a few days to dry, which was a good thing because my focus quickly turned to getting to know our new neighbors and Hughie in particular.

CHAPTER 19

Hughie Papworth, the Flat, and Nemahbin Lodge

THE BEING-A-KID PART of the summer really got rolling with Hughie's arrival. I could hear them calling to one another, and playing while I cranked the mulish water pump. It seems that moments of extreme frustration register more vividly in my memory. I confess to banging the gas tank with my fist that morning. I'd have picked up the whole assembly and thrown it in the river if I'd been as strong as the lumberjack folk hero, Paul Bunyan. It took no longer than usual to get the pump going and to raise the water pressure sufficiently, but it seemed like it took three times as long.

I remember hustling next door after finishing my chores to find five boys playing softball on the large flat between the two houses. Hughie said something like, "This is Tad. He lives in the ghost house next door. Let's play."

There was no formal introduction other than that. Hughie was the oldest and the leader of the pack. He directed me to right field, which put me last in the batting order. The left fielder turned out to be a cousin named Mickey Bliss. He and I were the same age, and Hughie was a year older. I was big for my age of fourteen and about the size of Hughie, who was bigger than his brothers and cousin. Hughie's brothers included, John who was a year or two younger than Mickey and I. Eddie was next, and Steve was the youngest.

My recollection about the rules is vague, but from what I recall the guy up only got one out. However, if he made it safely to first base, he returned to the plate and batted again. The rules were immaterial. The challenge was to get that rare hit that sent the ball out-of-play onto the outcropping where the house was perched. The house was out of range, but the icehouse and bushes on either side up on the bank were considered a mighty blast and earned a point. These competitions provided each of us with a full measure of fun, and after many more games in the weeks that followed, it was a reason for melancholy when the summer season ended.

I can still hear in my memory the sound of the dinner bell ringing. I was invited to stay for lunch. We sat at a giant picnic table on the lawn facing the back of the house. The house buffered the prevailing wind. It is no trick to remember where the table was, or its homemade wooden design. It was painted green, and it is still there as I write this, fifty years later.

Hughie's two sisters, Annie and Joy ate with us. They were the youngest and both brunettes. They were cute kids who turned into pretty women. At the time I took little notice of them. Boating, fishing and softball had my focus at that moment.

I asked Hughie if they went water skiing or toured around the river. "No ... We aren't allowed to run any of the powerboats," he said. I tried to hide my surprise because I was already learning to run *Buzz*. I wondered where this no motorized boat policy came from. Our family consisted of Mom, Dad, Deb, Betsy and me. None of our relatives or other cousins used the island except for rare brief visits. The Papworths had sixteen grandchildren, and about half of them were boys with a thirst for excitement and a deficiency in common sense. There weren't nearly enough boats to go around, and boats tend to be easy to break and expensive to fix.

They did have a double-oared skiff, similar to the single-oared *Bobby*, named *Helen*, and the younger generation was allowed to use her.

Hughie suggested he and I try some fishing since softball was over for the day. I hadn't had the opportunity to buy any fishing gear of my own yet, but spare gear was abundant at the Papworths', where fishing was another accredited activity.

As we walked toward the boathouse to collect our fishing gear, I remember Hughie informing me, "Our end of the island is known as Nemahbin Lodge."

I was a teenager, and I'd heard a lot of the island lore before we ever arrived. I knew that there had been a cut between the two islands that was upgraded to a canal with a stone wall liner that followed each side up to the level of the flat. Apparently a dead body floated into the canal around 1890. Great Grandmother Clark was horrified by this development, and she demanded the canal be filled in immediately. A steel peg was driven into a stone at each end of where the canal had been to mark the property line. Hughie pointed out where the shallow cut between the islands had run. I looked where he pointed through an opening across the flat, and I saw the main channel. Next he showed me the iron peg near the boathouse, which marked the back channel end.

CHAPTER 20

—— ✑ ——

Fishing and Surveying the Territory Too

EARLY ADVERTISING FOR the 1000 Islands, around the time when President Grant visited in the 1870s, characterized the region as a "fishing paradise." I never became addicted to fishing like many residents and visitors, but I did while away a number of hours fishing the first couple of seasons at Comfort Island.

My first angling outing with Hughie turned out to be a great way to become acquainted with more of the Papworth's property and some of ours' too. Hughie began the unofficial tour when we entered their boathouse to pick out our fishing tackle. I noticed right away that this was no simple shed to keep the sun off their boats, but a substantial building with living quarters overhead. The living quarters were built primarily on dry land adjoining the bank next to the steps that led to the main house.

The dockage consisted of one wide slot with a dock on each side. Numerous cleats and tying rings were spaced at convenient intervals to secure a small fleet of boats. I'd estimate the dimensions of the boathouse were eighteen-feet wide and fifty feet long. A long dock ran the length of the slip and then extended toward the New York shore and Keewaydin on the upriver side. This dock was at least one hundred feet long. A year-around seven-mile-per-hour current takes aim at any landmass facing the same direction as the side of Papworth's dock. It is not a wavelike assault except in spring when the river adds ice to the equation. Floating debris like tree limbs and an occasional runaway beam slam into the dock as well, but this sort of abuse is random and unpredictable. I remember the old dock well and I've seen pictures too. It was at least ten feet wide and made of wood at that time, but a half a dozen years later

Mrs. Papworth replaced this dock with a steel dock reinforced with cement that has resisted the elements ever since.

A large community room with an oversized round table in the middle was the essence of the first floor. A set of stairs at the end of the building nearest the main house was access to the second floor. On the side of the room opposite the stairway was a ground floor bathroom. The upstairs consisted of several bedrooms and a second bathroom. This facility provided overflow accommodations for the large numbers of family and other relatives who came to visit during the summer.

The outside dock was a preferred fishing spot. Looking up the river from the dock and this end of the island, I could see the International Bridge three or four miles in the distance. There stands a pyramid-shaped, cement channel marker about seventy-five yards from shore in the direction of the bridge. I remember swimming to that marker with some of the Papworth kids and Deb in answer to a challenge a few weeks later. The memory is a little foggy, but I've never forgotten how hard I had to swim to cut through the current. Only a small number of us, including Deb made it all the way.

Across the island on the other side of the Papworth house was another prime fishing spot. Looking to my right I saw our pump house. We cast our lines out toward the shipping channel where the prevailing current met the eddy and created little whirlpools. The fish could lie in wait where the current was neutral, and pick off various food sources caught in the current.

I recall pointing to a couple of black painted bollards that are shaped like mushrooms with an oversize torso as I asked Hughie, "What are these overgrown metal mushrooms for?" They were imbedded in the cement landing area next to the seawall.

Hughie explained, "They were designed for tying up ships or other large boats."

I suggested, "It doesn't look like any place I'd want to tie a boat" as wakes from passing boat traffic lashed at the jagged rock surface.

"See you for baseball in the morning, Hughie." I said as I headed home late that afternoon. I took the path on the other side of the flat from where the main path was. The main path runs next to the pump house and main channel. The back path follows the Keewaydin main shore. I hadn't had a chance to explore this part of the island yet, and I remember being anxious to see the buildings and area for myself.

I walked over to the edge of the flat to have a closer look at the little island. A seawall with a flagstone cap defined the end of the flat, and provided a clear passageway for about a foot of water that made its way down a narrow canal before reentering the back channel. A ramp constructed of two two-by-ten foot planks with treads to improve footing spanned the eight-foot corridor between the two islands. The dwarf island was mostly a pile of rocks and had a diameter of around fifty-feet. Very little topsoil was in evidence. I wondered how several bushes and a sapling were able to gain a foothold in this seemingly barren ground.

As I walked toward the path leading to our back porch, I crossed home plate in front of a small one-room shed with a door at each end. It required a step up to enter the building that was at one time the Comfort Island laundry. I thought back to Great Grandfather Clark's first guest book entry and the name of the Maria Morton who undoubtedly spent many hours washing clothes and linens in this shed. I noted a remnant of an antiquated boiler for heating water was lying next to the building.

The construction was board and batten. I spent some of my early years in Santa Barbara living in a board & batten farmhouse made from redwood. The boards were approximately ten inches wide and were placed vertically on the side of the building. In order to keep the building protected from the elements a thin strip of wood several inches wide, called a batten, covers the seam between the boards and thereby seals the wall. This was a popular building method for barns and outbuildings during the 1880s when the laundry was built.

Flourishes were cut into the window shutters in the shape of hearts, and a decorative curved design followed the wedge-shaped overhang at each end of the building. The Victorian influence was unmistakable.

I knew Dad had given Mr. Papworth permission to use the building as a shop in our absence, and it was full of tools, saws and other devices.

Next to this building and adjacent to the outlet of the canal was the icehouse, which needed attention even more than the main house. Several steps led me to an elevated door with a handle but no latch. I pulled the door open and looked down at the bare floor. I noted that the structure had double walls. When I got back to the house, Dad explained, "They built two walls with space in between in order to insulate the building, and that kept the ice blocks from melting too fast in the summer. Workers would come cut blocks of ice from the river during winter, slide them to the building and pack them in sawdust."

The approach to the back of our house was up a cement walkway that was much steeper than the front path. I remember mowing the grass on this slope with perspiration soaking through my shirt and the gas powered push-mower at the level of my chest. The steps were in worse shape than the front where I'd had a step give way on my first visit. I used extreme care climbing these steps testing each rung before moving to the next one.

An oak door on the left entered the utility room where we had discovered the ice tongs and kerosene lantern wicks. The stone chimney that serviced the coal Dockash butted up against the wall beside the utility room door, and an ancient wood box, once used for coal but now wood, was lined up next to the chimney. The back door leading into the kitchen was straight ahead from the top of the stairs and next to the wood box. The door was solid oak, but a ventilation window had been positioned above the door. The window was the width of the door and about eight inches high. The window pivoted open and shut on a metal peg that was seated mid-window on each end. These windows were located over many of the bedroom doors on both floors to create a breezeway on hot summer nights. I marveled at how cleverly houses were designed before the advent of modern conveniences like air conditioning.

⚬

CHAPTER 21

⚭

A Fishing Derby Papworth-style

DESPITE THE FACT that Grandpa Papworth was a gruff old codger, he did have a weakness for cats. He arrived at the island each summer with several barn kittens that quickly grew strong enough to control the rodent population. At the end of the summer season he returned the grown cats to the farm where he'd gotten them, or found them other homes. The senior Papworths went to Florida for the winter, and it was impractical to take several half-wild cats with them. The next summer he would get several new kittens and repeat the process.

I remember a picture of his jowly face as he looked through his bifocals at an adolescent black-and-white kitten that he had cradled in his arms. A rare trace of a smile, and the care with which he is holding the kitten caused me to suspect that there was a warm heart somewhere beneath his irascible exterior.

It was a few days after my first all-day visit that included softball, lunch and fishing that I arrived to find it was to be a kitty-oriented fishing marathon. This is one of my favorite island memories. Mr. Papworth passed out several coffee cans along with instructions, "Go to that big leaf pile adjacent to the stone icehouse and collect worms from under the leaves."

The building was a round one-room structure built with stone and about twenty-feet in diameter. This was the same icehouse we used for target practice in our daily softball games. Upon our return, I recall all of us arming ourselves with one of the many unpretentious fishing poles that had been accumulated over a number of decades.

Grandpa had filled a couple of buckets full of water while we hunted worms. Hughie and I placed the buckets near the prime fishing holes. The assignment was to catch as many rock bass and perch as possible in two hours unless Grandpa called a halt sooner. These little fish were plentiful compared to regional game fish like small and largemouth bass, pike and the rare muskellunge that weigh as much as sixty pounds. People didn't care about catching or eating the fish Mr. Papworth wanted for his cat food.

The fishing was downright simple. I would put half a worm on my hook and dangle my line over the side of the dock. A perch or rock bass would take the hook. I'd reel him in, take him off the line, throw him into the bucket and bait my hook again. These little fish were so abundant around the sides of the dock and seawall that it was hard to see past them to the river bottom.

The other kids took off after fishing, but I was curious, and I stayed to watch Mr. Papworth brew his cat-food stew. He had an outdoor sink and cutting board. I watched as he sliced the fish into small pieces and threw them into a large cauldron with meal filler. Next the cauldron was heated on a small stove next to boathouse until the contents came to a boil and turned into a thick paste. He placed the finished product into large pots that filled a special refrigerator placed outside the boathouse under the overhang. The fish were too small to make good eating for people, but the cats loved them.

A couple of weeks later we reconvened for a second Nemahbin Lodge fishing marathon. It's a testament to the event that I had just as much fun at the second event as I had at the first.

CHAPTER 22

⚭

A Bat Hunt and Other
Adventures With Hughie

A St. Lawrence Skiff is a rowing vessel between 18 and 22 feet long, about 4 feet wide in the middle and pointed on both ends. It weighs at least a couple of hundred pounds and is the perfect rowing craft for the strong currents and choppy water found in the 1000 Islands. Hughie had told me about their double-oared skiff called *Helen* during lunch at the picnic table. Following our softball game a few days after the fishing marathon, Hughie suggested that we take a row to town to load up on candy and see the sights.

The next morning – or maybe it was two mornings later – Hughie and I set out in the *Helen* to assert our independence. I remember kidding with Hughie about, "We don't need no doggone motorboat to cruise the river." We may have even made up a little song around this theme. Fact or fiction, I have no clear recollection of it now.

I was a captive to Dad's schedule, and I had no way to come and go when I pleased. The *Bobby* project was languishing, as I was too busy playing with the Papworths to complete the work that still needed to be done. I figured rowing to town in the *Helen* would be a good trial run to see how to go about maneuvering a skiff to a chosen destination. With Hughie to show me the ropes, I felt this would be a great learning opportunity.

I recall the whole fiasco vividly. Hughie and I started out by rowing up the back channel to get the feel of coordinating the stroking motion in unison. What "unison," I thought to myself. We clashed oars repeatedly,

87

and eventually splashed our way to the Upper Town Dock. The fact that we climbed ashore without falling into the water was a major accomplishment. The skiff is far more substantial and stable than a canoe, but they do tip and bob from side to side. I've had occasion to lose my balance when being careless. I don't recall anything about our shopping experience in town that day. Rowing to town on our own accord was the reason for my excitement, and I do remember that with a chuckle.

The softball games continued to be a daily occurrence, almost as predictable as the sunrise until most of the players returned home. Hughie was allowed to stay a few extra days, which made for a couple of more memorable events. I recall one morning when Hughie came and took a turn trying to start the water pump. "I'll crank for a while, and show you how to start that thing," he said with bravado. It wasn't long before he'd had enough and I cranked for a while, and eventually one of us got it started.

I was filling him in on our latest bat encounter the previous night where a rogue bat had met an untimely death when the furry creature had a collision with the strings of my tennis racket. He said, "Where do those bats hide out? I'd like a shot at swatting a few myself."

And so it came to pass that Hughie and I spent several hours in the attic up to our ankles in bat guano exterminating as many bats as possible. We took a long pole and a tennis racket up the narrow staircase past another of Uncle Alson's murals depicting a cartoon character tending his boat named the *I.O.U.* in front of the now defunct Thousand Islands Yacht Club. There were sheets hanging from the rafters far above that provided a cozy setting for an army of bats. We took turns poking bats from the rafters with the long pole, which would cause a few bats to take flight; whoever had the racket would swat at the bats flying around, and we had a bucket where we deposited the casualties.

Eventually we had our fill of this mayhem, and it was apparent that we wouldn't be able to eliminate all the bats if we kept up that pace for a month. I learned with time that bats provide a useful function controlling the mosquito population, and I stopped signing a death warrant each time one got loose inside the house. A fellow islander, who manufactured fishing equipment, gave me a fish net after hearing of another more recent infestation with the provision that it should be designated as a "bat net." It evoked laughter when I received it, but I learned to catch the bats thereafter, and I've evicted them out a convenient window ever since.

I'd been at Papworth's so much in recent days that the adults were beginning to think I was seeking adoption. Hughie would be leaving the next day, and I went to see what was on his schedule that morning. We were in the boathouse contemplating some fishing when Mr. Papworth strolled in on his way to town. He asked, "I'm going to town. You boys want to ride along?"

In unison as though we had rehearsed our reply, we said, "Sure."

Grandpa Papworth had a favorite boat that he used a preponderance of the time. His favored boat was quite similar to *Buzz* with a long narrow hull with easy access due to a lack of decking. The boat was named *Ixat* or "taxi" spelled backwards. *Ixat* had shared *Buzz's* leaking malady before Mr. Papworth cured the problem in his own unique way. He filled the bilge to the waterline with cement. Long-term this pretty much destroyed the boat, but it didn't leak at the time I had my ride. I had recognized Mr. Papworth as a practical man, but I hadn't recognized just how practical he actually was until I saw what came next.

We had a close call with an oncoming boat that swerved sideways to avoid being hit by *Ixat*. I recall wondering what possessed Mr. Papworth to not be more careful. I learned later that Ed was a founding member of the Syracuse branch of the United States Power Squadron that works in cooperation with the US Coast Guard Auxiliary. He not only knew navigation rules, but he seemed to be prepared to run over any boater that inadvertently failed to adhere to a rule.

His destination that morning was the hardware store. As we approached the dock, he said something like, "Step lively boys and man those lines."

We were instructed to wait in the boat, which was fine by me. I sat back in our tub of a launch in one of the somewhat decrepit wicker chairs and soaked up a little sunshine as I chatted with Hughie. I recall watching several islanders going down the dock with personalized leather mail pouches heading to the post office. I watched some folks enter the market near the dock and the pharmacy at the end of the block.

We were close to the end of the dock nearest the street. A gray lean-to with a corrugated metal covering and no walls was located at the edge of the seawall and it met the dock at a right angle. This was a bait concession stand with two tanks filled with minnows. Several fishermen came and purchased bait while we waited for Grandpa Papworth's return.

CHAPTER 23

ↄb

One Night at the Chalet Convinces Me

I REMEMBER BEING sorry to see Hughie leave, but I know I was anxious to launch the *Bobby*, and thus have an alternative source of transportation. Deb and I smoothed out the rough surface left by the dried putty with sandpaper. Next we pasted masking tape onto the line we'd drawn to coincide with the waterline. I figured a carefully defined waterline would give our bottom painting a more professional appearance when done. I stirred the paint, and we both had our own brush and a small plastic container for the paint. Rather than taking an end and both painting toward the middle, we reasoned that it made more sense to each take a separate side, and paint the whole thing that way.

I remember saying something like, "Deb have you noticed that this wood is so dry that it's like painting a sponge?" I lavished the paint onto the surface, and it soaked down into the grain before I could reload my brush. While I had hoped it would be a simple task getting Bobby back into operation, I realized then that it was a bigger job than I expected. We would need to get another quart of paint, and apply a second coat to seal the majority of the leaks. At least I had a sense that we were making progress.

Mom and Betsy were still at the Chalet, but there was talk of them moving to the island soon. Deb had spent a couple of nights with Mom, and now that Hughie had gone, it was my turn. Since Mom had some health problems, she was taking prescription drugs to control her conditions. Mom waited until five o'clock each evening to have her cocktails, but when there was a long delay before dinner, it made for a difficult evening. This was before doctors understood the compounded effects of mixing alcohol and medications, which in Mom's case reduced her ability to drink even in moderation without it affecting her balance and composure.

Dad dropped me off at the Chalet. Deb and Betsy took the car, and drove to Watertown to do some shopping. Watertown is thirty miles down the road in the direction of Syracuse where Hughie lived. Harry and Mary Champagne greeted me on their way out the door with their 180-pound Great Dane. They were taking a break from their concierge duties, and going for a walk around the grounds that included a farm and inland canals built by George Boldt, who had been a hotel magnate with properties that included the Waldorf-Astoria in New York City. He built a working farm near the Chalet and shipped produce to his hotel each day to provide his wealthy patrons with fresh food despite the metropolitan setting.

I have passed the Chalet for years, which helps to refresh my memory of the exterior that exhibited numerous porches, strips of wood inlaid into the stucco and decorative railings that evoked images of an authentic Swiss chalet. I can still picture the magnificent walnut stairway that led to the second floor where Mom was staying. This was one of those days that made quite an impression on me. Mom and I played gin rummy non-stop until it was time to get ready for dinner. Mom had wanted to teach me how to play Honeymoon Bridge, but I had no intention of being a captive in this setting long enough to learn the intricacies of that game. It would have been nice to sit on the porch, but the weather is fickle in the 1000 Islands even during the summer. I recall being forced back inside when the wind picked up, and it began to spit rain as the afternoon progressed. By the time we went to dinner it was raining hard.

We had long since gained the status of "regulars" at the restaurant. We had eaten there nearly a dozen times despite meeting Mom and Betsy at Edgewood and Pine Tree when everyone felt the need for a change of pace.

As was her custom, Mrs. Smith came by to check on us. I remember her formal manner of greeting patrons. It is rare that a hostess muffles a smile in favor of keeping her distance from the public, but I thought she had this down to a science. I began to wonder if smiling presented a health risk for Mrs. Smith. My memory of her exact looks is not vivid. I mostly recall her aura, which only seemed to brighten up when Dad was in attendance.

I recall Peter "Salad" offering his opinion about Dad's rapport with Mrs. Smith, "Mr. Clark, you are the only person I've seen who gets "Old Horseface" to cool it and relax."

Dad loved to talk about the old days, and Mrs. Smith had lived in the old days. She was perhaps twenty years older than Dad, and they developed a rapport relating their individual experiences with Dockash stoves. Dad would recount the latest triumph or disaster while our hostess listened.

I remember one conversation where Dad said something like, "I got the stove going the day before last, and Tad had plenty of water pressure in the tank. Deb was going to have the first Comfort Island bath in four decades, but after filling the tub she discovered the water was ice cold. A quick check under the house exposed the problem. A pipe had burst. We're still hoping for that bath and hopefully before a fifth decade comes and goes."

I rubbed my eyes in disbelief after I saw something I never thought I'd see. Mrs. Smith giggled.

Mom and I returned to the room while Deb, Betsy and Dad headed back to Comfort in the *Buzz*. Mom had an after-dinner nightcap and was getting wobbly, which I found to be very unsettling. I recall being awake most of the night while worrying that she might fall and be hurt. We survived the night without serious incident, but I became a vocal advocate of moving the venue to Comfort Island sooner rather than later.

Two days later Betsy and Mom did move to Comfort. I looked up the date in Dad's diary and found it was July twelfth. Before I had access to these diaries, I would have guessed that Mom and Betsy spent the entire two months that summer at the Chalet. When I reported my finding to Betsy, she was amazed to hear that their total stay off the island was only three weeks. She revealed that she and Mom played so much gin rummy and Honeymoon Bridge in those three weeks that she permanently lost her taste for card games.

Dad, Deb, Betsy, and I had made preparations for the move. I had worked on the lawn and beach. Deb and Betsy bought paint and curtains. Dad had supervised while Gerald Slate fixed assorted plumbing problems, plugged holes in the ceilings and performed general cleanup. Mom reluctantly agreed to a trial run.

CHAPTER 24

❧

Comfort Island's Irreplaceable Gem – the Front Porch

Front porch

MOVING MOM AND Betsy to the island was a simple event because most of their luggage was already at the island. We took their remaining bags the day they checked-out.

Betsy took over the second floor bedroom at the end of the hall across from the bathroom. A large window looked out at the baseball diamond and the Papworth's property. Two narrower windows looked out at the shipping channel over the same porch that ran in front of Deb's room.

Mom and Dad stayed in the room with the upstairs fireplace and a covered porch facing Alexandria Bay, but Mom's true niche was the front porch. I wonder now if a plaque should be placed there in her memory. She was content to sit and read for hours, all the while keeping track of who was coming or going and in which direction.

Boldt Castle from front porch

I came to regard this porch as one of several features that distinguished Comfort Island as an extraordinary setting. I thought of my tree houses that never offered a better vantage point or a more comfortable place to sit and relax. I've never tired of the bird's eye view of boats and wildlife that comes into focus from that site. It is simply spectacular. Wicker furniture, convenient tables and a railing with a story to tell are among the accouterments that made this venue more like a nest than simply a place to sit and rock awhile.

Mom thrived on company, a martini, and conversation when the "porch opened" at five. A cornucopia of fun and interesting personalities came to enjoy a libation and frequently stimulating conversation. Those demonstrating a strong attendance record included Deb and I, Peter "Salad," George Gerhardt, Bouie Arnot, Tom Folino, and notably, Trey Vars. Trey gets extra credit because at one time or another, he brought along a cast of characters that included Jim "the International Painter," the suave Charley Evans, who later became the mayor of Nags Head, and Dwight Chamberlain who was even then an authority on bird vocalizations.

I recall Dwight and Trey staying for dinner one night. It was dark by the time dinner ended, and Dwight provided us with a most unusual tour on his way to the boathouse. He summoned a chorus of our local owl population that hooted back and forth with him at some length.

Trey lived almost directly across the main channel at another mansion named Oak Lodge. He had a wonderful imagination when it came to having fun. For years he hosted an event called the "Finney Fest," which I once supposed was a celebration of life and high ideals only to learn that it was an excuse to spend a wild weekend at the river after the sensible members of the family had left for the season. In Trey's case it was a no-nonsense grandmother affectionately referred to as "Granny Goodwitch."

Mom and Dad never became even part-time members of the responsible, no-nonsense society, and they were still at the river when the much-anticipated Finney Fest took place in 1968. I was there too. This was a two-day "bash" and Mom and Dad fit right in. In Mom's case it was a real testament to her drawing power that a wide array of her porch "discussion group" made multiple stops at the house for conversation and liquid refreshments.

Having guest books that date back to Comfort Island's beginning and to all the intervening years as well makes for memorable reading. I found some interesting entries for the first weekend of October 1968. Charley Evans writes an entry on October 4th saying, "We have arrived in Alex Bay to celebrate the annual Finney Fest – starting with drinks at Comfort Island!" His is one of a half-a-dozen entries for that weekend. Barbara Wall adds, "Mrs. Clark – I love your <u>hat</u> collection!" The next day Cotting White says, "Finney Fest began with sub-zero weather and lots of minor mishaps along the road but really got rolling aboard Comfort Island with the Clarks and various finneys."

Cotting's comments reminded me that it might as well have been a winter weekend in light of the cold rainy weather. I don't remember if we sat on the porch or in the living room, but I do know that Mom was as comfortable entertaining in the living room as she was on the porch. She simply moved a few feet southwest to be in front of the warm fireplace. Seating was plentiful in both venues.

I would vote Mom as the greatest porch-sitter of all time. Trey would also make my front porch hall-of-fame along with Great Grandfather Clark, who made a novel modification to his favored seating location back in 1883. The original Comfort Island Clark garnered my vote following a conversation I had with Dad a few days after we took up residence in 1961.

I was sitting on the porch with Dad and I asked, "How come the four inch wide boards on the top of this railing are pitched like a rooftop?"

He explained that the purpose for this design was to keep the wood from collecting water and rotting as a result. Dad went on to share a re-lated tidbit of Comfort Island history. I hadn't noticed until he pointed it out, but one section of the rail was flat. Apparently one evening in 1883 Great Grandfather Clark placed his martini glass on the peak of the rail in front of his rocker and it toppled off to the ground below. Dad continued, "The next morning the story was that Grandfather Clark instructed one of his workers to plane that rail flat, and that he didn't care a hoot about the danger of rot."

AE Clark's custom railing

I found it reassuring to hear that Mom was doing her part to uphold the tradition set by the first wave of Comfort Island martini drinkers, and it became a curiosity for me to test that flat section for soft spots each summer thereafter by rapping on it with my knuckles. The railing is now 130 years old, and despite decades of neglect I have yet to find an area where the wood has even the slightest amount of give to it.

CHAPTER 25

❦

A "Commanding View"

Brittania passing island on way to Toronto

MOST VISITORS RELISH the commanding view of the main channel and the cornucopia of boats, ships, and other watercraft that pass within easy viewing distance. There are a few that crave a tranquil and remote setting, and they take issue with the energy and activity surrounding the Comfort Island location. Expanding the St Lawrence Seaway in the 1950s opened the waterway to much larger ships that transport goods to and from Midwestern ports. Before the seaway was enlarged, the previous maximum ship length was two-hundred-and-fifty feet with a draft of fourteen feet. When the Seaway was completed in 1959, the size limit grew to seven-hundred-and-forty feet long, seventy-eight feet wide and a draft of twenty-six feet.

Ships pass within two hundred yards of the Comfort Island porch on a daily basis and occasionally much closer, as was the case with the 730-foot Jean Parisien on October 10, 1981. The Toronto Marine Historical Society reported that the vessel was "downbound with a cargo of Lake Erie coal for Quebec City when, about 6:15 a.m., in a heavy fog, she struck Comfort Island, bounced off, and then went hard aground on the rocks of Stony Crest (Jewel Island), just off Alexandria Bay, New York. With considerable hull damage, the PARISIEN took on water and soon acquired a sharp list to port."

The captain and several members of the crew stayed on board while the others retreated to Comfort Island. Seven of the crewmembers signed the guest register and then make an executive decision to open the bar since none of the Clark contingent was there to offer them a dollop or two to calm their nerves.

These freighters have carried many cargos including grain, oil, various types of ore, automobiles, and more recently containers and wind turbine assemblies. One of the primary carriers is Canada Steamship Lines whose fleet includes the previously mentioned *Jean Parisien*. The corporation has painted their ships with a distinctive reddish-brown hull offset by white pilothouses and superstructures. Their ships have passed by so frequently that I quickly recognize the names *Laurentien*, *Richlieu*, and *Frontenac*.

In 1967, I recall that we climbed the stairs to the tower roof for a better view of Her Majesty's Royal Yacht *Britannia,* but in most cases we have confined our viewing to a front row seat on the porch. Binoculars are as common to the porch tables as a coffee cup or water glass. The cruise ship *South American* was another regular visitor until 1967 when she was decommissioned.

Not all the traffic was spectacular like the 415-foot *Britannia* or the 290-foot *South American,* but the array of luxury and historic boats that have passed the Comfort Island porch constitute a dazzling parade of remarkable vessels. Celebrations of tall ships in places like Bay City, Michigan and Toronto, Ontario provides the incentive for large numbers of these square-rigged sailboats to pass Comfort Island in profusion. Charter yachts like the 377-foot *Luna* and Malcolm Forbes' 151-foot yacht *Highlander* visit the area in addition to many others.

The Highlander was a corporate yacht that had a few added touches like a helicopter and two tenders consisting of a 22-foot Donzi and a 19-foot Cigarette. The short list of guests invited aboard the Royal Yacht *Britannia* included Elizabeth Taylor, Mick Jagger, Presidents Eisenhower, Reagan, Ford and Clinton. The spectacle continues even today with the fully restored 138-foot steam yacht *Cangarda* headed ten miles upriver to Clayton's Antique Boat Museum. The expense in time and funds to restore this yacht was thirty men working for eight years at a cost of twelve million dollars. I did the math and that's an average of fifty thousand dollars per man per year.

Most of the boating traffic is rather pedestrian when compared to the vessels that cause me to reach for my camera. In our first years back at Comfort we mostly thought about another not-so-fancy boat that we could count on to get us to shore and back.

CHAPTER 26

❦

We Need a Reliable Boat

FOR ISLANDERS BOATING is a necessity. For sportspersons, vacationers and outdoors enthusiasts, recreational watersports is the reason most visitors come to the area. My observation is that summer boating, and pleasure craft activity has become more popular with each passing year. I've not only watched, but I have also been an active participant in exploring the river. I've watched fishing boats and pleasure craft darting in and out of the channels between and around the myriad of nearby islands. I have found the constant flow of action to be quite remarkable.

Mom thrived in this porch setting, and I recall sitting there with her on a regular basis.

Just because the five of us were now living together at Comfort, it did not mean that we ate many of our meals there and that applied to dinner in particular. Whereas we ate at the TI Club most of the time out of convenience when Mom and Betsy were staying there, I remember branching out more after they left.

I recall going to Pine Tree Point quite often despite the old folks bias. The view was spectacular, and Dad loved going there. He would chat with Cap Thomson who would recount the Ginger Ale story and renting his dog to Great Grandfather Clark with each visit. Deb, Betsy and I routinely asked to be excused after we finished eating. While my two sisters poked around the gift shop or took a stroll, I'd go looking for Preston who was the head bellhop and an accomplished Ping-Pong player. The resort had a table downstairs, and we'd play until Deb or Betsy came to say we were leaving. I remember Preston, and the fun we shared like it was yesterday.

As soon as I moved to Comfort, I realized how important it was to be able to run a boat. In Santa Barbara I could walk to the nearby village, or ride my bike anywhere around town. It was a little over a mile to Alexandria Bay, but there was no walking or riding a bike to that destination.

I signed up for a safe boating course shortly after we arrived. From what I remember, classes met twice a week in the evening, and the course lasted three weeks. We learned about right-of-way rules, navigation markers, safety equipment and other useful information relative to having fun on the water without endangering others or ourselves.

About the time this class was concluding, I had the ride to town with Mr. Papworth where we narrowly avoided a collision. Because I was taking this class, I knew Mr. Papworth was probably holding his course because he had the right-of-way. When we were in danger of having the collision, I had a first hand example of an unwritten rule my instructor, Dave Rogers, advanced about the use of common sense. Many boaters do not know the rules. If we had collided and one of us had drowned, it would have been the other driver's fault, but someone would still be dead.

I found an entry in Dad's diary saying I scored 100% on the certification exam taken on July 13th. This meant that I was licensed to operate a boat without an adult on board before I reached the age of fifteen.

Dad often let me run the *Buzz* when we went someplace together. I had run the boat home at night several times, and I understood the principles of docking from practice at the river and from my boating experience in Santa Barbara before we came to the river. Being on an island leads to a lot of boating experience unless it is at the Papworths' where the development of boating proficiency was not part of the curriculum.

Being licensed to run a boat is one thing, and having a reliable boat to operate is another thing altogether. Many decades ago I made the observation that if boats were planes, there would be no such thing as flying. I continue to stand by that observation. I have broken down in boats more times than I can count.

I recall the cold and rainy afternoon when Dad broke down on the way home from town. I found the reference in his diary. It was June 21st, which happened to be the day Deb, Dad and I moved to Comfort. A neighbor from an island beyond Papworths' stopped and gave Dad a tow home. It was clear Buzz was not a very reliable boat. After Mom and Betsy moved to the island, the need for a more dependable boat became a primary concern.

The local weekly newspaper, the *Thousand Islands Sun*, ran ads for the various boat dealers and individuals that had boats to sell. I remember each of us scoured the latest edition of the paper that week in mid-July searching for the perfect new boat. Dad's diary explains that he, Deb and I went to get coal for the stove in the nearby community of Redwood. On the way back we drove to Schermerhorn's Marina in Chippewa Bay. The marina was several miles further downriver from Pine Tree Point. We went to take a look at a perspective boat for purchase. The boat was a sixteen-foot Thompson with a windshield and a bench seat adjacent to the steering wheel. The wooden hull appeared to be well built and in good condition, but most important it was powered by a new 40-HP Evinrude outboard motor.

Several days later the decision was made to buy the boat. I remember this unique event well because buying anything with the word "new" attached was out of character for Dad. In the years I've been a summer resident of the 1000 Islands I remember many incidents where people have perished as a result of boating carelessness and mishaps. Dad also remembered families being wiped out when someone failed to use good judgment. Buying a new reliable motor got my vote as an example of Dad doing the smart thing.

The importance of this acquisition became immediately apparent when Dad ran the *Buzz*, with the whole family on board, the seven miles to Chippewa to complete the transaction. Chippewa Bay is a treacherous stretch of rocks with a little water here and there. Rocks were lying in wait in unlikely spots like just below the surface in open areas without any islands in the vicinity. Dad bought a chart of the area at Rogers. I recall being the navigator and talking to Dad as we made our way through the gauntlet of rocks toward Schermerhorn's Landing. "Dad I can't see which way to turn this confounded map to get an accurate fix on where we actually are. This chart shows rocks all over this area." I said.

"I know what you mean. Try turning the chart a little one way or the other in relation to something like that island over there." He said pointing at a nearby cottage off to our right. We crept forward, but before we arrived, *Buzz* conked out. It's referenced in his diary, but I remember without any assistance. A couple of fishermen came to our aid. One fellow knew enough about engines to solve our problem by using a bit of sandpaper to remove residue from the "points." It was none too soon to add a second more reliable boat to our island transportation resources.

CHAPTER 27

───── ❧ ─────

The Beach, Makeshift Docking, and Evenings at Comfort

I REMEMBER THE first time I explored the beach area. Up on the grass above the sand I found a pile of rotting wood. As I examined the mound more closely, I noticed several sections of boards had ribs attached. This appeared to be the skeleton of a boat. I asked Dad and he said, "I think that may be the remains of the original one-cylinder *Comfort*.

Apparently there were at least two small launches with one-cylinder engines used by workers and the caretaker at the island. The function of these launches was primarily to run errands, or to get to work and then back to shore at the end of the day. The construction was similar to the skiff, *Bobby*, but the hull and ribs were a little more substantial to support the motor and the shaft that spun the propeller. I had a ride in the sister ship, *Medora*, a few years later. I recollect feeling insecure with the lack of freeboard, and it took a very long time to go even as far as the mile to town.

Someone had pulled the *Comfort* up on shore and removed the motor long before my first summer at Comfort Island. Each day I was gaining a greater appreciation of what happens to things left to the elements for long periods of time.

The beach was another treasured feature of what made the Comfort Island location so special. Natural sand beaches are rare in the 1000 Islands region. This particular beach was a product of being at the foot of the island where waves and current wouldn't wash all the sand away. What current there is sweeps across the beach in the direction of the main channel. A granite ledge known as "toothbrush rock" acts as a barrier to keep sand from advancing past the beach area. The "toothbrush rock" title dates back to the 1880s, but I don't know if it was simply a figure of speech, or if the first summer residents, actually started off their day brushing their teeth at that handy location.

In addition to the sand on the beach there was an abundance of black shale material. Dad explained, "That is the residue from the spent coal used by the *Mamie C* steam yacht." I thought back to the photo I'd studied so often in Dad's office with steam billowing out of the whistle as it sat at the dock next to the beach. I realized the engineer had obviously shoveled the spent embers into the water at this convenient site. I found an unexpected form of recreation with this debris. The thin flat surfaces of the embers proved to be a functional shape for skipping these projectiles on top of the calm water.

Swimming was big at both ends of the island. At the Papworth end, we'd dive off their long dock, splash water at each other, throw beach balls or tennis balls back and forth, race from here to there and or maybe simply drift around on inner tubes. At our end the younger Papworth kids had an open invitation to come with an adult to swim and play. There were toys, the sand, and shallow water to play in without contending with the deep water and dangerous currents that existed at the upriver end.

Indeed the beach provided good swimming for folks of all ages. The gradual deepening of the water was great for the little kids, and our dogs could wander in for a drink or a swim without the danger of being unable to get out. A short swim away was the toothbrush rock ledge that had a flat surface extending toward the main channel. I often stood on the flat area before diving in and swimming around or back to shore. Photos and text entries abound with references to all of us congregating at the beach to sit or swim. This was another choice vantage point to watch the action on the river.

I remember Dad thought the beach might work as a possible parking spot for our new more reliable boat. "Tilt the motor up Tad, and we'll see how the boat does up on the beach." Dad and I pulled the bow up onto the sand and then tied the bow line to a nearby tree. After a couple of days it became clear that any sort of wave action was grinding the boat's bottom. The coalhouse dock was only long enough for the Buzz.

Dad and I checked out other possible landing spots. Despite the fact that the boathouses and docks surrounding them were gone, we noticed one section of the cement seawall that held promise. A pair of wooden beams ran parallel to the waterline along the length of the cement. The water depth was adequate for a span of fifteen feet or more. If we had a way to protect the side of the new boat from the cement dock, we'd have a solution to parking a second boat.

I have the luxury of several photos that detail our makeshift dock, and a July 24th entry in Dad's diary where he mentions us fabricating the dock. We found one-by-six inch staving boards once part of the old docks in a woodpile next to the coalhouse. We nailed the boards in a perpendicular position relative to the horizontal seawall beams. These boards cushioned the boat from the cement. What we had devised was actually a better place to land than the coalhouse dock where Buzz was tied up.

With Hughie gone and Mom and Betsy now in residence, I recall doing more as a family. While we went out to dinner often, we also stayed home a few times. Dad was in charge of the Dockash coal stove. I don't recollect if we bought the wrong coal in Redwood, or if it was simply hard to start and keep going. What I do remember is that it was a consistent disappointment. If we had counted on that stove to cook dinner each night, we'd have been placed on the starvation-watch list. I only recall one night when Dad kept the stove going long enough to heat the hot water for Deb's bath that turned ice cold when the hot water pipe burst.

Not much was salvaged from the apartment over the bigger of the two boathouses that had been torn down before our return, but a kerosene stove did find storage space in the back hall off the kitchen. Dad and I moved that stove into the kitchen, and we used it for the rest of the summer. I recall one night when a north wind was blowing, and it was pouring rain too. No one wanted to go out in that weather so Deb and Betsy cooked corned beef hash in a skillet with fried eggs on top. The stove had three or four burners and that was plenty for our needs.

Comfort Island was built long before instant entertainment magically materialized with the flip of a switch. One of the living room closets was stocked with cards, dominos and other assorted games. Dominos became a favorite for Mom and me. We would keep a running total of our score. We might play to fifteen hundred or two thousand points before we'd start a new game. I don't recall how many sessions it would take to reach those totals, but we did have fun. We mostly played before dinner, but occasionally we'd play after dinner too. Some of the score sheets still exist, which assists my memory in recalling those events.

CHAPTER 28

❧

A Few More Memories of My First Summer

1961 photo of family at top of stairs

DEB AND I worked sporadically on the *Bobby*, and I read in Dad's diary that we launched her on Mom's birthday or July 29th. I recollect it took Gerald Slate, Dad, Deb, Betsy and me to wrestle the craft down to the beach where we put her into the water to see if Deb and I got a "pass or fail" on our efforts to make her watertight. We had to wait a couple of days for the results in order to give the water that rushed in a chance to swell the wood, and hence tighten the seams. I recall Deb and I pumping the water out after a few days and then noting, "Look Deb the leaks have slowed to a trickle." We now had another means of transportation to add to our growing fleet.

I found old black and white photos from 1961 that document me taking Mom, Betsy and Deb for several rows in the channels surrounding Comfort. Rowing a skiff is relatively easy although working the oars took some getting used to. Each individual oar fits over a pin on the gunwale, and the handle extends in front of the person rowing. Rowing a skiff is tricky because the handles overlap in the middle of the boat. It took me a while to coordinate the motion of bringing the oars back together without having them wedge together. One oar needs to be in front and the other right behind it. Then I'd dip them into the water and off I'd go.

The easy part of rowing a skiff is it goes where it's pointed, and it glides a long way once it gets going because it is quite heavy. As Hughie and I learned, skiffs are not easy to land because the nine-foot oars get in the way near the dock. Having rowed dinghies, canoes, kayaks, and other self-powered rowing or paddling conveyances, I rate the St. Lawrence Skiff my favorite.

It was possible to explore inner bays and other channels too narrow for a wider hull or a deeper draft. I was able to float right over rocks and shoals to get a close-up look at the size and shape of these unseen hazards.

As for the house, I had neither the tools nor the skills to work on that monumental project. What a laugh. It took a contractor and a team of workers four years to return Comfort Island to a remote semblance of respectability. Nonetheless that did not keep me from developing an interest in building projects toward the end of the summer after Hughie had left.

I remember building a surfboard a few days before we launched the *Bobby*. I took a couple of two-by-ten inch planks that were nine or ten feet long. I discovered the materials in one of several woodpiles. I can still see it. I sawed the front to a point and added some Red Lead bottom paint for cosmetic appeal because leaking wasn't an issue. I recall padding down to the next island one afternoon. The current was between seven to nine miles per hour, but I'd been training on the Pacific Ocean five days a week by riding waves between two-feet high to twelve-feet high. I was a very experienced swimmer, and the school I had graduated from that spring had a PE program that began and ended with twenty minutes of swimming before lunch each day at the public beach. However, as a senior citizen, I'd consider such a trip foolhardy today lying on a crude pair of boards while attempting to navigate the turbulent water that is now vastly more congested with a huge increase in the number of watercraft in general including fishing boats, jet skis, and runabouts, which scamper in and out of the interconnected channels that circle this concourse of islands.

Dad had lots of memories from his youth on Comfort Island too. I recall one day when Dad and I were collecting wooden shakes that had fallen off the roof. We were piling them under the front porch when he mentioned one of his early memories. I remember him saying something like, "I used to build sailboats with old wooden shingles like this when I was a kid. I'd carve one end to a point like the bow of a boat. Next I would drill a hole in the middle where I'd place a mast made with a straight stick. Finally I'd take a sheet of paper and punch two holes in it so it would fit over the stick in the shape of a sail."

He went on to explain that he and his cousins would take their shake sailboats down to the canal adjacent to the flat and conduct races.

The memory was a obvious catalyst for Dad and me to build a couple of prototypes and proceeded to the canal to test them out. I recall the details well. We launched our sailboats at the same time from the ramp to the small island. The ramp bowed toward the water with the two of us squatting on it, and this made it easy to place our boats into the leisurely current simultaneously. The wind followed the course of the canal and caught the sail of each boat propelling it forward. Thirty feet or so down the canal I waded into the shallow water to retrieve our two boats so we could begin the next race. It was a fun and memorable experience Dad and I shared that day. I made a mental note to introduce this sport to Hughie and his competitive brothers when we got together the next summer.

Our dinners at Edgewood uncovered an interesting association with a college student who worked at the registration desk. He was a personable young man, and he would greet us on our way to the dining room. He showed an interest in our decision to return to the area. He voiced his hope that we would be able to restore Comfort Island to the regal state he envisioned. I recall the evening when he told Dad, "My name is John Comstock. My grandfather was Captain Comstock who piloted your family's steam yacht, *Mamie C.*" I thought to myself, here's another "it's a small world" surprise. It was almost certain that it was his grandfather blowing the whistle on the *Mamie C* in the picture that was so much a part of my memory before we came to Comfort in 1961.

Our list of dinner restaurants was expanding beyond the core list of the TI Club, Pine Tree and the Edgewood. The Homestead was becoming Dad's new favorite and an addition to the list. Unfortunately both the food and the atmosphere were deemed to be second rate by everyone else in the family. Having a newer more reliable boat was an excuse to venture further from home in search of a good meal without being paranoid about becoming stranded with boat trouble.

We heard rave reviews about a restaurant named Heffernan's. It was located on a Canadian island named Grenadier about ten miles downriver from Comfort. The chart we had used to go to Schermerhorn's Marina conveniently included the area where the restaurant was located. It was necessary to round an island downriver then skirt a prominent pile of rocks while motoring up a narrow bay surrounded by wetlands that included mostly cattails and water lilies.

I have forgotten some of the details, but other details are still vivid. Dad squeezed into a space on one of the two docks, and Mom, Betsy and Deb went to put our name on the list for the first available table. Adults brought their own alcoholic beverages if they cared to drink, and as I recollect the restaurant provided tea, coffee and water for those who did not drink. The menu was simple. Fried chicken, aged Black Diamond Cheese, corn, potatoes and apple pie with ice cream were the basics, and they made sure no one went home hungry. I remember walking up an access road behind the restaurant while waiting for a table. The dirt road opened up into a field of corn. A couple of barns and a farmhouse were on higher ground at the far end of the field. This was the Heffernan farm where they raised the chickens and vegetables for the restaurant.

It was a special place. I was glad I got to see it before the Heffernans retired and moved on the next year. Mrs. Allen and her husband, Walter, took over the business. I enjoyed numerous fun evenings with them in charge too before they closed the doors in 1974.

We left the river on August 7th to take a tour of the East Coast. Dad and Mom had planned a trip to parts of New England and a number of major cities including Boston, New York City and Washington DC. The trip included many stops. We eventually reached Chicago, where Mom, Betsy and Deb took a flight back to California for the winter.

My first summer at Comfort had reached its conclusion. I remember thinking back to my optimism when I signed the guest book upon our arrival. I realized that my initial burst of innocent enthusiasm about making Comfort shipshape in a few weeks had quickly given way to reality. I had removed sticks and limbs from the lawn, cut the underbrush that covered the walkway to the coalhouse where we tied *Buzz*, and I raked leaves into open gaps in the seawall. I also pruned some of the overgrown lilacs and other bushes. I bought a large scythe to cut the tufts of grass that were once the lawn, but I soon resorted to a grass whip, which worked better and was easier to use. I raked some of the coal residue from the beach and filled in sections of the eroding seawall with the lose shale material.

Overall my efforts were akin to vacuuming the house. The yard looked better after I did it, but it needed another going over a week or two later to maintain the improved appearance. I did get some of the coal residue off the beach, but there is still a lot left after fifty years and many additional sessions of removing the embers.

I had more fun than I'd ever had before in two summers. Santa Barbara was a special setting, but the 1000 Islands was even better. Being a few steps away from a beach, fishing or boating was fantastic, and in the coming years I'd see how it could get even better.

I had my first taste of becoming a "river rat." I didn't know what the term meant at the time, but I have grown to know and appreciate what it is in the fifty years I've been migrating here. It is many things to be a river rat. It is the sound of the ducks, geese and osprey issuing their calls. It is the flow of the river as it gurgles and gently slaps the shore on its journey to join the Atlantic Ocean in Nova Scotia. It is a call heard by those of us who cannot escape the magic of this unique setting. The pull and allure of the mighty St. Lawrence River had grabbed onto my psyche forevermore.

CHAPTER 29

— ❧ —

Indian Lore, Tour Boats, Modernization

THE INDIAN HERITAGE and lore in the 1000 Islands is mostly forgotten as the twenty-first century moves inexorably forward. Keewaydin State Park, Chippewa Bay, and Iroquois Island are reminders that the Cornwall brothers, Cap Thomson, and the Clarks have no claim to being the region's earliest residents. Indians had a hand in naming or lending their name to many places found along the river. They also provided the names for the mighty "muskellunge" fish and the "muskrat," which is the critter that gives rise to the term river rat.

When Great Grandfather Clark landed with his family and servants in 1883, Indians were still coming to camp on the plateau across the back channel at Keewaydin. It was a mythical setting for the Algonquin Indians. The 1000 Islands had sacred status for the Iroquois and Algonquin tribes. At least one account credits the Indians naming the 1000 Islands "Manatoana," which translates as "Garden of the Great Spirit." James Fenimore Cooper makes references to "that labyrinth of land and water, the Thousand Isles" in his novel the *Pathfinder*. I found a reference to this encampment in a 1936 *Thousand Islands Sun* article that was reprinted and edited by Jeanne Snow. There is reference to the Keewaydin property and the owner at that time, William T. Dewart. In one section of the article it is reported, "There is a bit of Indian lore told about the spring on this property. It was here that the Indians used to camp and to use the water from this spring."

Early Clark lore details an evening when the braves had something important to celebrate late into the night. They were apparently drinking something stronger than the renowned spring elixir, and they were creating quite a stir according to the account. As the story goes, Great Grandmother Clark suggested Great Grandfather Clark roust the care-taker and row over to parlay a truce about late night noise levels. Quiet was restored. My theory has been that the senior Clark promised a ship-ment of top shelf "firewater" as soon as the family returned to Chicago if the braves would quiet down for the rest of the family stay.

I have wondered how it came to be that the tribes ceased coming. Had the area become too commercially important to share space with Indians? Whatever happened they soon disappeared from the scene, and in 1894 a wealthy individual, J.W. Jackson from Plainfield, New Jersey, built a grand mansion on the Keewaydin site across from Papworths'. In 1961, New York State acquired Keewaydin, and it became a State Park thereafter. Ironically, camping returned to this same scenic spot that the Indians had once occupied. Park officials continue to strive even now to keep noise at civilized levels.

I have found numerous arrowheads in various locations but never any at Keewaydin or on Comfort Island.

Tour boat excursions began in the 1000 Islands well before 1900 with steam powered vessels. The industry continues to provide an important source of commerce to both United States and Canadian communities along the St Lawrence River shoreline throughout this region. Alexandria Bay, Clayton, Gananoque and Kingston all had tour boats that passed Comfort Island a number of times each day. It continues to be a lucrative business one hundred and fifty years after it originated. Dad and other local residents often referred to this species of craft as a "rubber-necker boat" since the passenger's heads were in constant motion looking one direction and then another.

A captain steers a predetermined course through a variety of scenic island groups. An announcer or in some cases a recording mixes fact and fiction about who lives where, what led to their prosperity and other assorted tidbits of information that might be of interest. It is not hard to imagine that Comfort Island had become a favorite place to get a laugh from the passengers when the announcer would point to our house, which no longer had any paint while saying, "These people are paint manufac-turers, believe it or not."

I took one of the Uncle Sam Boat Tours in August 1962 during my second summer at Comfort Island. Cap Thomson acted as the co-announcer for one or two tours each week that season and as I recall Deb, Betsy and I went to-gether on his tour. The boats were of wood construction during that period. Passengers boarded through an entrance at the stern then filed down a cen-ter aisle with wooden bench seats situated on both sides similar to a bus. The captain piloted from a seat in the bow, and an announcer had a loudspeaker system to provide details along the route during the tour. The *Uncle Sam* that Cap Thomson preferred for his tours was built in 1926. It was sixty feet long and ten feet wide. It was single level, and it had glass windows about two feet high and three feet long running the length of the seating areas. It was a handsome boat with a white hull and a varnished above-the-gunwale structure, which supported the windows and a wood top.

My memory is vague about most of the spiel, but there was a sto-ry about each of the mansions we passed. When we came by Comfort Island, Cap Thomson skipped joking about the Clarks' being paint manu-facturers, but he did talk about the ginger ale he choked on there and about renting his dog to my great grandfather. He completed his Comfort Island spiel by pointing toward the porch while saying, "I see Mr. Clark on the porch. 'Hi Mr. Clark. I'm tellin' these folks about you rentin' my dog and the ginger ale story.'" I had to laugh when I made a quick calculation that placed Great Grandfather Clark's death more than fifty years before the tour that day.

Jewel Island is the next island downriver from Comfort. This was the island the Seaway Authority dynamited in half to make room for the larger boats that would be navigating the Narrows. To this day the story about the Seaway consortium purchasing the property remains unchanged, "They paid seventy-seven thousand, seven-hundred, seventy-seven dol-lars and of course seventy-seven cents."

Mrs. Papworth told me a story about a tour boat passing close to her shore, while an announcer pointed at her and said, "This is where Mary

Pickford lives." He even went so far as to greet her, "Hi Mary." Her name was Mary (Papworth), but she wasn't from Toronto, Canada, nor was she ever a silent movie star.

The previous summer had mostly been a matter of Dad mapping out a strategy for upgrading, restoring and rebuilding. Restoring the roof was Dad's top priority. Mom's first request was to bring electric power to the house. A boathouse was on the rebuild list, but financially that project would have to wait.

As I look back on the 1961 summer, I realize why Mom and Dad opted to take a tour of the East coast rather than stay longer at the island. From my point of view, we were in survival mode the first year. Keeping the water going, the bats out of our living quarters and buckets under the leaks was more than enough to keep each of us busy. The inevitable days of rain and cold were simply too inhospitable inside the cold damp house. Our two boats were ill equipped for venturing out in foul weather, which made it very unpleasant getting off the island to take refuge somewhere else.

I noted from Dad's diary that we didn't arrive at the island until the last day of July in 1962. This arrival date made sense to me because workers would be busy in and on the house from April through July.

The Papworths already had an underwater electric cable brought to the island. A transformer was located on the flat between the two houses, and that device supplied power to their property. The electric company determined that the power supply was adequate to furnish both houses. Dad made arrangements during the 1961 summer for the Niagara Mohawk Power Company to bring power to our property in the spring of 1962. Dad contracted a local electrician, Fred Dobbins, to do the basic inside wiring. It took some clever work to hide the wires on top of moldings, and to find routes to various rooms through small holes in the lath and plaster walls. It wasn't a fancy wiring job because the house would have needed to be gutted to accomplish that task. That would have been a monumental job, and it would have destroyed the murals we all wanted to preserve.

Dad also contracted with local builder Perry Simmons in the fall of 1961 to reroof the house before we returned for the 1962 season. The roof had been allowed to deteriorate for such a long time that the contractor didn't need much more than a broom to remove the few wooden shakes that had somehow clung to what was left of the old roof. Reroofing the house came none too soon as we found out several decades later. In our 1990s restoration project, we found rot so advanced in the porch soffits that sawdust was all that remained under the covering boards. This rot was clearly a product of the roofing neglect from 1925 - 1961.

CHAPTER 30

Hughie, Boating, Island Romance

HUGHIE AND HIS brothers had nearly finished their stay when we arrived. Our first morning softball game was August 1st. This was less than twenty-four hours after we arrived at the island. I don't recall spending nearly as much time with Hughie in 1962 aside from a very scary boating mishap. I had use of the *Gibson Girl* outboard most of the time. Hughie had joined me for a ride, and we were idling along near the Papworths' front seawall that faced the main channel. Hughie asked if he could run the boat for a few minutes. When he took over the controls, he mistook the throttle for the gearshift, and we took off at full speed into the rock wall in front of us. It was a miracle that the bow climbed the rock surface at an angle and then dropped back into the water when he managed to pull the throttle back to idle. It took more than a few minutes to stop shaking, and even today my heart rate accelerates when I think of that incident.

I gained a greater appreciation for why it's important for anyone spending a significant amount of time on an island to be taught the rudiments of how to operate a boat. It was not a case of the Papworth grandchildren being forbidden to run a powerboat. They were simply not allowed to use any of the senior Papworths' powerboats. Hughie's dad had a triple-cockpit wooden speedboat named *Black Knight*, but it was a substantial craft that wasn't well suited for teaching young people how to run a kid-friendly boat like a small outboard. As it was, Hughie's dad maintained the same no-powerboat policy as the senior Papworths. Hughie's cousin Skip Fryer brought his own little outboard the next summer, and he had the freedom to use it as he pleased.

Hughie was a good friend. We had lots of fun during my first summer in particular, but we grew apart mostly because we were not at the island at the same time for any extended period except for 1961. He married and raised a fine family. I've seen him a few times, but it is rare. He gets around in a kayak whenever he goes boating now.

Two days after we came, Dad added another boat to the growing fleet. He bought a 1939 Chris-Craft Utility launch that we named *Comfort*. Having a third powerboat made it convenient to send *Buzz* to Rogers to have the bottom replaced. At the same time Rogers was working on the *Buzz* bottom, Deb, Betsy and I were working in shifts on Dad's one-design sailboat. His sailboat, *MT*, had found a temporary home with his Yale classmate, Andrew McNally. Mr. McNally had two boys and a girl. Some or all of his kids used the boat before they graduated to power boating and water skiing.

The *MT* had a history dating back to the mid-1920s when Dad and other members or guests of the Thousand Islands Yacht Club were participants in sailing races. The Thousand Island Class, Knockabout, also known as a Thousand Islands one-design, was designed by John Alden and built by Chaisson Boat Builders of Swampscott, Massachusetts. Outfitted with a mainsail and a jib this 15-foot vessel was equipped with a centerboard in order to help the sailor maintain control despite the River's swift currents and tricky wind shifts. The 6-foot beam provided extra stability for dealing with unpredictable wind gusts that swirl around the myriad of islands.

A sense of community developed among the principles and sometimes a fledgling romance might take root. Dad's recollection of that period was expressed along the lines of, "There was plenty of excitement associated with the arrival of these six newly minted Thousand Islands one-design sailboats. After I named my boat the *MT*, Clover Boldt, named hers' the *QT*." Names like Dewart, Haydon, Shumway, Eggleston, McNally, Boldt, Kincaid, Berdan, Hammond, Oliphant, Rafferty, and others shared the camaraderie of those carefree days.

However, life can change quickly and often without warning. A scant three years later in early 1928 Mancel Sr. unexpectedly died of pneumonia.

He had been a catalyst for these races providing the committee boat and presiding over many of the regattas. In 1929 the stock market collapsed and the Great Depression followed. The TIYC languished during the 1930s. Robert Mathews reports in his concise history of the "Thousand Islands Yacht Club" that the property was sold for taxes in 1944 and torn down two years after. The *MT* languished too, but it survived.

The hull was leaning against a shed when we began our restoration work. We followed a similar procedure that had worked when we sealed the bottom of the *Bobby* the previous summer. We cleaned the bottom and removed as much old paint and chipped caulking material as possible. We pressed new caulking into the seams before repainting the bottom, sides and deck. Like the *Bobby*, the job took more time and work than we anticipated. According to Dad's diary, we launched the *MT* and towed her to Comfort Island on September 4, 1962.

Perhaps the *MT* had a mystical attraction that Dad alluded to back in the days of the *QT* and the Thousand Islands Yacht Club. The *MT* played a cameo role in my first 1000 Islands romance that summer. About the time Hughie left for the season his cousin, Martha Fryer, arrived. I remember being attracted to her right away. What was the nature of this attraction I wonder now as I look back? She had a talent for making the most of her appearance and personality. I recall her warm greeting. I found her slender figure and blond pixie hairdo added to her allure. I wanted to get to know her better. Even though she was a few years older than I was that didn't seem to be an impediment. Quite the opposite, she expressed interest in lending a hand on the *MT* project.

Working on the *MT* with Martha became a reality a few days following our introduction, but we also spent some extra time working on a second boat restoration project. I remember well driving Mom's outboard home after we put a coat of paint on the *MT*. I suggested extending the ride by touring the islands near the TI Club where Mom and Betsy had stayed the previous year. When we came to that point where it was her dock or my tour, we both tugged the steering wheel. Much to our mutual surprise the mahogany dashboard split in half. The lower half landed in our laps. We unexpectedly had a united purpose of fixing the *Gibson Girl* before our folly was discovered.

In the process of repairing our mishap, our smiles, laughing and kidding around made it clear to us that our fondness for one another was growing. I had grown out of the stage of being shy and uneasy around a girl that I found attractive. While I had moved on to seeking idyllic romance, the idea of sex and romance was not even on the horizon yet.

I remember she had dinner on the dining porch with us one evening following our boating incident. Several days later Mom and Dad had a cocktail party that included the Papworths in addition to numerous other neighbors and friends. I treasure the memory of taking a walk down to the canal adjoining the flat with Martha as the party was winding down. It seemed only natural when we shared a lingering kiss.

Martha had a serious boyfriend back home, and the next summer reason prevailed. She married her sweetheart at the island, and was gone from my life and has never returned. I would relish reliving those tender moments with her. I have reflected how on occasion my path has crossed another's for only a brief spell, and yet sometimes those moments are some of my strongest memories. I recall a bit of Eastern philosophy that presented an explanation that has resonated as a truth to me ever since, "The soul knows not time, only growth."

CHAPTER 31

⚬

The Dining Porch; Another
Comfort Island Gem

Site of many parties; the dining porch

THE DINING PORCH, where Martha joined us for dinner in August 1962, was another gem like the beach and front porch. Each of these embellishments contributed to making the Comfort Island setting something extra special. A ten-foot wide veranda surrounds most of the house. The front porch wraps around both sides of the building. The side facing the pump house and main channel runs the length of the structure and even extends around the back of the house and the master bedroom. On the Keewaydin side the porch borders the living room and dining room. The section of porch adjacent to the dining room is dominated by screening that provides an open-air dining venue, which is inaccessible to mosquitoes and bats.

An outdoor variety of painted wainscoting was attached to the original railing enclosing the bottom three feet of the porch. Screens built in panels were fitted into the openings between the top of the wainscoting and the porch roof. Screen mounted to wooden supports from floor to ceiling along with a screen door sealed the front porch end of the area. A side door connected to the dining room accessed by a short ramp completed the enclosure.

The first-floor windows that look out to the front porch and the dining porch were built in two sections. The bottom section had two panes of glass and measured a height of six feet. The upper section had one pane of glass and measured three feet. Taking the bottom six-foot section of the window closest to the kitchen and putting it on hinges created the door that led into the dining room, thus providing access to the butler's pantry and the kitchen.

There were mounting brackets for kerosene lamps on the posts supporting the roof and more brackets on the exterior dining room walls too. Dad found electric lamps that had an antique appearance with semi-translucent white ceramic shades and chimneys that fit over the light bulbs. These lamps were in keeping with the Comfort Island motif, and as an added bonus the mounting arm of the new lamps fit the kerosene brackets. Dad also liked to enhance the atmosphere by lighting one or two of the old kerosene lamps, which he placed in the brackets on the house exterior.

A single pane window with a wide white molding in keeping with the other porch windows acted as a pass-through to the butler's pantry. Next to the glass entrance door was a button in a recessed casing that was hooked to a buzzer in the kitchen. In days gone by a primitive battery was hooked to the circuit to trigger the ringer, and thereby summon the kitchen staff.

I'm not sure when the dining porch table arrived on the scene, but it was a stout oak table with several leaves that we added during the outside dining season. It would comfortably seat eight, and I recollect instances where we seated ten or more. It was four feet wide and rested on central supports with elongated feet radiating diagonally to the floor for added stability. There was no shortage of chairs in the house. A set of ten varnished wooden chairs with caned seats have been used for dining purposes ever since I first ate there in 1961.

During the early and mid 1960s, we frequently ate on the porch as a family. Deb and I spent as much time as possible at the island while Betsy split her summer between school and the island. Dad's diaries support my recollection of Betsy generally coming to the island for about a month each summer. I recall that we often had guests from around the river community join us for dinner as couples or as individuals. Houseguests have been a tradition at Comfort Island from the beginning, and we would convene on the front porch and at the dinner table to catch up on the news. The guest books are teeming with entries of friends and relatives that came to enjoy the river and the island. The entries of our company continued to fill new pages and new guest books.

The screened enclosure kept the mosquitoes out and contributed to long relaxed dinners. I recall sitting at the table chatting with friends, relatives or simply family long after dark. Comfort Island had a sizable bird population. A family of wrens became long-term residents of a convenient post supporting the roof next to the screen door. A piece of wood had fallen out of a connecting joint, thus providing an entrance to what became a cozy nest. They are still returning each season as I write this in 2013. These and other birds chirped their goodnights as dark approached. Outboard-propelled boats added to the evening sounds as they traversed the back channel. Dad liked to refer to these boats as "the mosquito fleet" in a tone that conveyed his annoyance that someone would be so inconsiderate as to disturb the tranquility of our pristine setting. In more recent years campers at the Keewaydin State Park have provided a pleasant backdrop of kids in particular expressing their joy of being outdoors and on vacation in such a splendid location.

Wren habitat in dining porch beam

Not all evenings were tranquil and relaxed, however. I remember one bizarre evening when we gathered as a family including Betsy. That particular evening featured an unscheduled visit by a resident bat while we ate. This happened on occasion, and I'd either chase it out the screen door or go on the attack with my tennis racket. This was before the advent of my bat-net that I used in later decades to expel wayward bats unharmed. The bat in that particular instance didn't leave peaceably so I fetched my tennis racket. The scary looking, fierce little creature dive bombed the four family members eating to a chorus of shrieks before I connected with an overhead smash that terminated its earthly existence. The miscreant sailed the length of the porch before colliding with Dad's forehead, whereupon it fell onto his plate just as Dad was about to carve another bite of his meal. The expression on his face, and in fact all of our faces, were surely classics. I recall Dad saying, "I was about done eating anyway. Now I know I'm done"

Mom and Dad generally hosted an annual cocktail party. This custom originated in 1962 with the party that Martha and the rest of the resident Papworths attended. The dining porch served as the bar area, and the dining table was crowded with plates of crackers, dips, peanuts and other munchies. This porch in combination with the front porch provided ample room for dozens of guests. I have an old photograph of one of the early parties that jogged my memory. I was surprised to see that the men both young and old were wearing skinny ties and suits or sports coats. The women were all wearing dresses.

Parking was an issue when having a party that required advance planning. Rafting-off or tying boats side-by-side is one solution for docking more boats when space is limited. Climbing from one boat to another when rafted off is tricky business and best left to the young and agile. The younger set that included my group of friends did fine with this maneuver, but for the more elderly guests, we made arrangements with neighbors like the Papworths to park overflow boats at their dock. We would save a dock space where the person piloting the boat could let their passengers off before proceeding to a nearby location to park. In some cases I remember using a second boat to follow an individual who parked at another island.

The Comfort house rests on top of an outcropping, and the walk up the hill will raise the breathing rate of a fit athlete. For women in high heels and their stepping-out threads or senior citizens in general, the walk up the hill was best accomplished at a sauntering pace. It produced quite a scene from the porch watching men and women making their way up to the house in all their bright colored finery.

I used to claim that if I wanted to see everyone at a party, I could do so by standing next to the bar. The bar was usually the first stop before the partygoers moved off to small groups or one-on-one conversations. It was a diverse group that attended our parties. The guest list included members of the rich and famous, eccentrics and artistic types. I enjoyed visiting with many interesting individuals. The conversations ran the spectrum from river issues to current events, history and good-natured repartee. Gradually the party would wind down and tranquility would return.

The 1000 Islands party dress code has definitely relaxed in recent years. Dresses, ties and coats have been replaced in most cases by shorts, skirts and button-down shirts. Most of the old guard is gone and along with them a slower paced more genteel day and age.

—— ✿ ——

CHAPTER 32

Relatives, Houseguests and the *MT*

PROVIDING ACCOMMODATIONS FOR family and guests has never been an issue at Comfort Island in my years going there. There are five large second-floor bedrooms in the main upstairs section of the house that still have original tin numbers affixed to their respective doors. The numbers read "two, three, four, seven and eight." In the 1880s there were apparently eight numbered bedrooms. I don't actually remember being told that the bedrooms with the missing numbers were in the attic, but I do know the attic had sleeping cubicles back in the days of Great Grandfather Clark. The upstairs bathroom had hooks corresponding to eight bedrooms for the purpose of towel management. The numbered rooms did not include the maids' quarters where three more bedrooms are located. There is a master bedroom and bath downstairs with an adjoining room that could have served as a bedroom too. These rooms are not numbered either.

Beginning some time around 1930 the bats took over the attic. It would take a major cleanup and restoration effort to turn that area into suitable living space again. Not having the attic as overflow sleeping space has been of little consequence. Suffice to say there has been adequate room to accommodate half a dozen houseguests at all times during my tenure. I have no recollection of anyone coming to stay during the 1961 season, but both Deb and I had a friend come to visit in 1962.

My friend, Peter Schramm, from Santa Barbara came to stay the final two weeks of the 1962 season. We made several trips to the McNally complex to put the finishing touches on the *MT* and when we completed the work, we towed it back to Comfort Island. Peter and I wrestled the mast into the slot designed for that purpose, and I connected the stays that keep the mast stabilized. Dad rigged the sails with help from Hutchinson's Boat Works. Peter and I went sailing. The wind was moderate at perhaps five to ten knots blowing in the prevailing direction or downriver.

The boat had a centerboard, a mainsail and a jib. I had been to sailing school in Santa Barbara, and I understood the rudiments of sailing. There is considerable current flowing downriver on both sides of Comfort Island. I remember reasoning that it would be best to sail upriver to see if we could make headway against the current. Peter manned the jib while I managed the mainsail and the tiller.

I recall being amazed by the way the *MT* handled in what I regarded as difficult conditions. The wide six-foot beam made the craft more stable than I had expected despite winds that were gusting and swirling. The centerboard gave the fifteen-foot craft surprising traction against a four - to-seven mile per hour current. Before I knew it we were well past Papworths' and halfway to the International Bridge a couple of miles up the main channel. Peter had scant boating experience, and he looked back at me several times in a way that expressed concern and uncertainty particularly when wind gusts caused the boat to heel over abruptly in the early going. As we sailed on, it was apparent that the *MT* had been designed specifically for the conditions we were facing. It wasn't long before we were both laughing and chatting about what a blast it was to sail such a fine craft.

I spent numerous hours sailing the *MT* alone in the years that followed. I sailed downriver most of the time because the river widened in that direction, which made for more scenic tours and better sailing too. I remember one time when I had sailed several miles downriver in the northeast direction that the river flows and then west toward the Canadian town of Rockport. I was quite a distance from home when the wind dropped to near zero. I was worried that I wouldn't be able to make it home. Bucking the current near the Narrows adjacent to Comfort Island heightened my anxiety, and I recall looking back where the tiller and water met. A flicker of wavy motion that trailed behind me provided some reassurance that I was indeed moving fast enough to produce the basic characteristics of a wake as the hull moved sluggishly through the water. It was slow going, but I was able to make headway through this challenging section. If the *MT* had been a dog, I'd have given her a hug and a cookie when I reached our dock. In 2011 I donated the boat to the Antique Boat Museum, where I knew it would be preserved and perhaps reproduced for use by future generations.

Dad's cousin Alce Ann Cole was his Uncle Edwin Clark's daughter, and as I recall, she came on a yearly basis for a number of years beginning in 1969. Late in life Alce Ann became an avid photographer. She was intrigued by the history of Comfort Island, and she documented both the exterior and interior by taking eight-by-ten inch, black-and-white photographs. I remember numerous occasions when she set up sophisticated lighting and screens to illuminate the background for her photos. Alce Ann had an eye for the flourishes that highlighted the Victorian era like ornate doorknob designs, decorative moldings and banister carvings that appealed to her eye. She assembled separate collections of pictures of the house and all the outlying buildings in several large cloth bound folders. She exhibited her collection in the San Francisco area where she lived and donated the second collection to the Comfort Island archives. Dad collaborated with her on a brief history of Comfort Island that she had printed in the form of a four page, letter-size brochure. This brochure displayed a large photo of the house on the cover, and the written contents served as an introduction to the photographs.

I'm not sure how Dad's father ended up as the sole owner of the island, but comments by Alce Ann and her nephew, Edwin Clark III, caused me to think that her side of the family may have had some reservations about not being part owners. Dad welcomed Alce Ann and Alson any time they cared to visit, and surely he had nothing to do with any ownership issue. I've wondered about the unspoken undercurrent I sensed at that time, but I'm relatively sure I'll never know with any certainty since all the members of my grandfather's and father's generations have passed away.

Dad's cousin on the Alson Clark side of the family was named Alson like his father. It was his father who was the impressionist artist that painted the murals on the interior walls. Alson, the artist, had passed away in 1949. I was at the late toddler stage, and I have no recollection of him. His son had a fine wit that made for some fun repartee with Dad. For example, our hot water supply was challenged in the days when Alson and his wife Carol visited. I recall one morning when Alson had been second in line to shower. Dad asked him how his shower was, and Alson responded saying, "It's a clear case of the early bird getting the warm."

Other relatives came to visit, but not with the same frequency as Alson and Alce Ann. Numerous memorable evenings were spent dining and conversing together on the screened porch. It was an opportunity to get a better feel for the early days at Comfort Island, and to learn more about some of the lore I've been able to share.

Mom and Dad had a number of friends from Santa Barbara come for a visit too. I recall their close friends Hamilton P. Greenough and his wife Helen coming to visit in 1967. Helen was my mother's best friend, and Hamilton was a very eccentric individual with roots in Boston. Hamilton had graduated from Harvard while Dad had completed his college degree at Yale. Dad and Hamilton liked to banter back and forth about the college rivalry in particular. Mr. Greenough was worried about flying so they took the train. He carried a rope and hammer just in case the train had some mishap that required extricating himself by breaking a window and lowering himself to the ground with the rope. I was not there during their visit, but for many years we enjoyed the use of the glasses they sent as a "thank-you gift." The glasses are 14oz. tumblers with a royal blue rim and crossed burgee flags of the Thousand Islands Yacht Club and the Clark insignia flag.

CHAPTER 33

~

Exploring the River

My mobility around the river had taken a leap forward on Labor Day in 1962 when for my birthday, I received the *Gibson Girl* as a gift from Mom and Dad. The sixteen-foot craft had originally been intended for Mom, but she found maneuvering the boat to a dock and then grabbing the dock quickly was too difficult for her to manage. I had been given permission to use the boat most of the time prior to it becoming mine. Nonetheless I regarded the difference between taking my boat and borrowing Mom and Dad's boat as a subtle but important difference.

I remember the day I received *Gibson Girl*. It was my sixteenth birthday. I looked at the boat as I approached the dock. The lapstrake hull, with each board overlapping the board below it, was painted white. The windshield framing and decks were varnished. A cleat for the bow line, a chromed horn and running lights were necessary accessories for operating or securing the vessel, and they were located on the front deck.

I was quite excited as stood next to the boat and surveyed the interior. The flooring consisted of plywood painted gray. The rest of the interior was a light shade of varnish with the ribs exposed. I gazed at the dashboard, which brought back memories of the secret kiss I shared with Martha and how we had replaced the split dash a week or two before. A top was attached to chrome tubing that gave shape to the canvas and stabilized the assembly. The rolled-up canvas and tubing fit conveniently in front of the steering wheel and dashboard next to the windshield.

When needed, it was a simple task to unfurl the canvas and snap it to the fasteners on the windshield. The entire region surrounding the 1000 Islands is dotted with lakes and tributaries because it rains a lot. Anyone counting on a boat for transportation needs a top.

I was becoming more independent. I began exploring the river, and made new friends. I liked the idea of a wide range of acquaintances rather than conforming to a small clique of friends. I found that many island groups and areas of the river had kids about my age. It is hard to imagine how large and spread out the 1000 Islands are. There are eighteen hundred islands spanning fifty miles of United States and Canadian waters. There are many areas and diverse groups of people I have yet to meet. It would take months if not years to visit every cottage on the islands and shoreline.

The 1000 Islands is a seemingly endless maze of islands, bays, inlets and obscure channels in such profusion that a neophyte on river geography could easily get lost. Now that I had my own boat, I would take a couple of charts, like the one Dad and I used to navigate the route to Chippewa Bay and later to Heffernan's Restaurant, and I would go exploring. On many occasions Deb would come along too and read the charts looking for shoals as we motored through tricky sections.

I remember one time in particular when Deb and I were exploring a narrow channel between two islands with a swift current pushing us forward. Midway through the channel we realized we would surely hit bottom if we didn't back up immediately. I put *Gibson Girl* in reverse and opened the throttle. There was an interval when it was a stalemate whether the 40-horsepower motor would be able to buck the current. I felt the tension as I gripped the gas lever as tightly as possible as though that would give the engine extra power. After what seemed to be an excruciatingly long pause, the boat began to inch backward. I had an adrenaline rush that left me shaking after we were clear from further danger. Other times I recollect getting disoriented in unfamiliar areas at night. I would slow to a crawl until I found a landmark I recognized. The 1000 Islands can be a very dangerous area, and I learned early on to go slow at night and most of all to respect the river.

CHAPTER 34

⚬

Making New Friends and Water-skiing

IN THE IMMEDIATE area I had the Papworth kids and Trey Vars to pal around with. However, by 1964 I had branched out and was routinely spending my days with Pieter Bergen and Rhea Inglehart, or the Thomas kids water skiing. I found Rhea most attractive, and although we never became an item, we did become good friends. Rhea and Pieter resided a few miles away near Lake of the Isles while the Thomas family were another mile or two further downriver on Tar Island. As it turned out, I later married Rhea's cousin whose family had a summer cottage across from Tar Island on Grenadier Island. Both of those islands are in Canada.

I was introduced to Rhea and Pieter because my parents socialized with their parents. This was not the way I met many of my other friends. My fascination with exploring the river was partly motivated by my desire to meet other kids my age. If a saw a group of kids water skiing, I'd get my courage up and stop to ask how the skiing was going and thereby introduce myself. When I noticed a pretty girl as part of the contingent, I was twice as likely to stop to say hello. I met the Thomas kids on Tar Island this way and the Smith girls on Estralita Island too. Like throwing a rock into the water, the waves rippled outward. I took the first step by boldly introducing myself. This led to meeting them and their circle of friends, which led to making more friends until I eventually knew many kids.

Pieter and I were determined to become proficient water skiers, while Rhea had knee issues that limited her participation. The *Gibson Girl* only had a forty horsepower motor, which wasn't sufficient power for faster skiing or for doing tricks like skiing barefoot. I remember using the *Comfort* for some of our skiing before Dad traded the outboard for a sixteen-foot Gar Wood Junior, which had an inboard motor and more power. Pieter and I spent hours practicing the basics of getting up efficiently, skiing across the wake and then jumping the wake. It wasn't long before we developed a passion for mastering slalom skiing. I wanted to ski all the time during that period.

The Inglehart family knew it was lunchtime when I arrived. I recall a typical day at the Inglehart's. I would arrive about noon dressed in a T-shirt, bathing suit and bare feet. I'd breeze through the screened porch where Rhea's father, George, was generally found reading in his favored wicker chair. He was a New York Supreme Court judge, and I remember greeting him with, "Morning, Judge." He'd usually look up briefly to confirm that I was barefoot, which was one of his pet peeves.

I recollect him chuckling while saying, "It must be lunchtime." I felt honored that he tolerated my miscreant behavior without taking issue. It probably helped that he and his wife, Paula, were close friends with my mom and dad. Whatever the reason, I certainly appreciated a tasty lunch on so many occasions.

Once I had enough food stowed away to fuel further activity, Rhea and I would cruise across the narrow channel to Pieter's houseboat. Even though the Rodier houseboat was only a slingshot distance away, it was in Canada whereas the Inglehart cottage was in the United States on the Wellesley Island shore. The fact that the border was so close became a non-issue for me after a while. The International Rift is a short distance from this location. I could have thrown a medicine ball from one country's shoreline to the other at the entrance to this cut between Hill Island, Canada and Wellesley Island, USA.

The *Amaryllis* was no average houseboat. It was one hundred feet long and had a second deck on top of the first. It was built in 1911 and served as a residence. A verandah, dining room and living room with a fireplace meshed nicely with four bedrooms upstairs that all had full baths. Pieter and his mother, Bunt, lived on the houseboat. She and her unscrupulous husband, Pierre Rodier, were friends of my parents before Pierre absconded with a considerable percentage of Bunt's fortune.

I did not know about Bunt's problems at the time. All I knew was that despite being a couple of years older than Pieter and Rhea, we had fun sharing each other's company.

CHAPTER 35

_____ ❧ _____

How About a Row?

I WAS CAPTIVATED by the challenge of learning to navigate the St Lawrence River within a ten-mile radius from Comfort Island.

Geologists say that the 1000 Islands were formed from an ancient mountain range that has been whittled down to their present size over millions of years. I know of no island of the eighteen hundred in this chain that has an elevation of more than a hundred feet or so, and there hundreds and perhaps thousands of would-be islands that never were prominent enough to rise above the water surface. Just below the surface these rock obstructions lurk in wait of the unsuspecting boater. Areas like Chippewa Bay, Thousand Islands Park and Ivy Lea are notorious for their rock-infested waters.

Hundreds of island clusters, coves and tricky channels within a ten-mile radius were hard for me to comprehend. When I added learning the location of a thousand hidden shoals to the observable landscape, I realized the scope of this task was monumental. I spent many days and countless hours scouring various areas to plot routes I could take for the pleasure of cruising or simply to reach a desired destination. I prided myself in knowing my way around many scenic and often tricky sections of the river.

I'd take my outboard and follow tour boats and other larger boats to learn new sections. I used charts to explore other areas upriver and down. I gradually developed various routes and tours I liked to repeat, and one tour I came to enjoy more than others was the route around the big island across from Comfort Island or Wellesley Island. It is a good twenty miles to circle Wellesley. I had heard stories about fishing guides rowing their customers long distances in the days of my great grandparents. A few in-dividuals during this 1960s period reported rowing around Wellesley, and I liked the idea of adding my name to the short list of those accomplish-ing this feat. Toward the end of August 1965, I launched *Bobby* from the rowboat slide and began my attempt to row the full way around.

I had decided to go the more difficult route against the stronger cur-rent upriver to the head of Wellesley. The main channel going upriver had a variety of summer cottages dotting both the New York mainland and Wellesley Island too, but there are no more than a few islands here and there. The Canadian side of Wellesley Island is quite different with a myr-iad of islands many of which are in clusters. The setting on the Canadian side was more tranquil and cottages were less abundant.

In rowing a skiff, you have to look over your shoulder to see where you're going and mostly you see where you have been. There is a rhythm to this long-distance rowing. I remember the feeling of the muscles in my arms, shoulders, back and legs applying a pulling pressure to the oars stroke after stroke at a pace I was able to maintain for a span of perhaps fifteen or twenty minutes without resting briefly then repeating the pro-cess. Aside from the squeaking of oars moving back and forth in the oarlocks, rowing is a quiet and solitary activity. The scenery passes by at a speed that invites study and contemplation. On a row of this length much of my time was spent in a sort of meditative trance while I focused on maintaining an efficient pace and the desired direction. However, I do recall seeing ducks, loons and herons. The waterfowl are inclined to go about their business as the skiff glides close to the wetlands where they are found in greater numbers.

There is a trick to rowing against the strong currents of the St Lawrence River. The guiding principle is that there is a current that goes counter to the prevailing current called an "eddy" that is located near the shore. I took advantage of this phenomenon and made good time.

In keeping with my long-standing knack of showing up at the Inglehart household just in time for lunch, I recall beginning my attempted cir-cumnavigation shortly before eight that morning intent on keeping my dubious record in tact. I figured the Inglehart's' cottage on Laundry Point was two-thirds of the total distance.

It was a nice day to row aside from boat traffic that featured the Gananoque Tour Boat fleet. The boats had burly wooden hulls and powerful motors, which produced speeds approaching 20 mph and potentially damaging 4-foot wakes. Some of the tour boat captains of this era had questionable reputations based on their lack of regard for shoreline property and other boaters. Boats throwing harmful wakes are expected to slow down when passing near docks with vulnerable boats tied up, and it's considered a courtesy to avoid violently rocking small fishing or pleasure craft that are parked away from the main navigation routes.

From the very beginning of this row, several of these tour boats deviated from their normal course and sped past me so close I could almost touch them. I couldn't tell if the captains were laughing and making a game of seeing whether they could tip me over or pour water into my boat, but I found no humor in having to ship my oars and hang-on as they passed.

At the head of Wellesley Island there is a narrow cut at the entrance to Eel Bay with Murray Island upriver. I was in the middle of this cut when another Gananoque boat barreled toward me. Instead of moving aside, I turned my skiff sideways blocking their passage. Being an unpowered craft I had the right-of-way, and the captain had to throw his boat in reverse to avoid hitting me. He cursed at me through his open window and his deckhand-announcer came out on the deck to insult me further. I stood up holding one of the two 9-foot-long oars like a baseball bat. I was prepared to knock the fellow senseless if given the chance. The deckhand scrambled back inside, and I had a few choice words of my own for the captain about boating etiquette and the "rules of the road" before letting them pass.

After four hours of steady rowing I arrived at the International Rift, which is a narrow channel between Wellesley and Hill Island (Canada). This channel, the width of an average shot-put throw, defines the international boundary and the water rushes through the opening in the direction I was going. A short time later I arrived at the Inglehart's dock.

I remember my conversation with Mr. Inglehart quite well that day. I opened with a typical greeting, "Morning, Your Honor."

"Lunchtime is it?"

"It is Judge, and I'm hungrier than ever as I'm attempting to row around Wellesley Island today."

Judge Inglehart looked up from the *New York Times* and chuckled as he said, "You could join a select club of those that have accomplished that feat. I did it myself a few years back."

My body craved nutrients, and I recollect that lunch tasted better than ever as I refueled for the conclusion of my "rowathon." Even though I felt the successful completion of the journey was a foregone conclusion, I still had a surprise ahead. As I rounded the foot of Wellesley Island, the anticipated stronger oncoming current greeted me, but what I hadn't expected was a stiff headwind that was getting stronger and impeding my progress even more than the current.

The last few miles were the most difficult of the whole trip, and it was nearing seven hours of rowing when I took the last few strokes and glided into the Comfort Island dock. My back was stiff and, despite my youth, my hands, arms and shoulders made it clear that I'd endured a strenuous challenge.

I reaffirmed on this outing that a skiff is as good a method as there is for learning the intricacies of the river both above the water's surface and the unseen obstacles that lurk in the shallow depths below.

∽

CHAPTER 36

The First Restoration Continues

DURING 1963 AND 1964 summers, restoration work continued at the island. Dad hired Ronald Shutler and Jon Short to work on the house in 1963. Jon only worked for us that one summer whereas Ronald assumed caretaker duties through 1967 when he returned to farming. Ronald had grown up on a farm in nearby Hammond, and like many young men who grew up on farms, he was a tireless worker who possessed the desirable trait of staying on task.

I have a photograph showing Ron and Jon painting the front steps while a pair of neighbors and my sisters are painting the lattice. I recognized the date of this "painting party" as August 17, 1963. Dad makes reference to this event in his diary. It was the same day Dad and Mom's hosted their second annual cocktail party.

Ron and Jon came to work while I was at summer school near Lake Chocorua, New Hampshire. I fell victim to the "sophomore slump," and consequently needed to make up a couple of courses in a six-week session at the High House venue. When I returned, I learned Jon had taken on the assignment of painting the tower by default.

I asked Ron, "Why aren't you doing some of the tower painting too?"

"I'm tending the ropes for the boson chair and when Jon drops a brush like he did yesterday, I lower a new brush to him. He also sends the empty paint can up to me when he needs a refill."

"Couldn't you get the job done quicker if you both painted?" I asked.

"Probably, but I developed a overwhelming fear of heights after I fell thirty feet off a grain silo a few years ago. My leg has never been the same, and I'm lucky it didn't kill me."

I can't deal with heights either, and I marveled at Jon's ability to complete that project. He was thirty or forty feet off the ground, but because the house was perched high up on an outcropping, it seemed much higher.

The fact that the sun-bleached exterior was getting a fresh coat of paint was a welcome sight to our neighbors, but the tour boat community was less observant or simply hated to see a favored part of their spiel go out of fashion. I recall several instances when Ron and Jon waved paintbrushes and paint cans at passing tour boats as the announcer recited the rehearsed lines of "these people are paint manufacturers, believe it or not."

Dad had many notations in his diary about the sequence of projects that Ronald and Jon worked on. After painting the tower and third floor dormers, they moved to the second floor where they made repairs to the antiquated windows in addition to painting the cedar shake siding. They replaced boards on the back porch decking, refurbished screens, and painted the first floor exterior including porch ceilings and railings. It was a busy summer, and the cosmetic improvement was extraordinary.

Ronald returned as the caretaker in 1964 and Jon moved on to other pursuits. Restoration projects were winding down with the exception of a new boathouse that was erected over the course of that summer. Perry Simmons, who had contracted to reroof the house returned to work in concert with Ronald on this endeavor. It took most of the summer, but when the job was done, we had a place to keep our boats out of the weather, and it also provided storage space for some of the boats in the winter.

The slip was forty-feet long and sixteen-feet wide. Dad's love of the past was evidenced in the boathouse construction like every other project I can think of at Comfort Island. Some old windows from the original boathouse had been stored in the attic where the ten thousand bats supplied babysitting services for sixteen years. Dad thought the windows would be in keeping with the island motif after a little sprucing up.

A general characteristic of Victorian era craftsmanship is flourishes and lots of labor intensive work. The windows consist of a central pane of glass a foot wide and a foot-and-a-half high surrounded by a dozen smaller windows six inches wide and between six and eight inches tall. Fabricating or repairing one of these windows is a long and tedious task, but when Comfort Island was built the going wage was a dollar a day.

Comfort boats in boathouse

The yard had been civilized again and Comfort had regained some respectability. Grass seed was added to the tufts of grass that had survived the decades of neglect. Scrubs and trees were trimmed and some of the seawall got a new cement cap.

My conscience demands that I divulge that not everyone on the island was delighted with the progress being made at the previously forsaken mansion. It was during this period that a pest control service was hired to provide a solution to the bat infestation problem. They plugged many of the avenues the bats used to come and go then they burned some powerful incense that resulted in a mass exodus of the furry little creatures.

Many years later "Mrs. Pappy" shared her secret with us. "Ed and I were sitting on our glassed-in porch that afternoon. At first we thought we were experiencing an eclipse. We stood at the door and to our surprise we realized that an army of bats was invading us. They took to our eves, the boathouse, and any other nook or cranny they could find."

This event underlines the fact that even the best of neighborly relationships have their trying moments.

CHAPTER 37

— ❦ —

Venturing Forth at Night

IT'S FUN TO imagine an idyllic evening cruising slowly on the moonlit water with a sweetheart at one's side, and there were occasions for doing just that, but for the most part that is a scene from a Hollywood movie. In reality boating at night is reason to be alert and to exercise caution.

Living on an island poses a different set of transportation obstacles than does being in a conventional setting on the mainland. It is necessary to operate a boat each time one wants to go some place. Walking is not an option and swimming ashore would be both dangerous and foolhardy. Running a boat at night is not like driving a car either. Boats are not normally equipped with headlights and there are certainly no roads to follow. Boats are equipped with running lights to alert other boats of their presence and location. A red light is attached to the left side of the boat, a green light is placed on the right side, and a clear globe with an illuminated bulb is displayed with 360-degree visibility at the stern.

I found it quite strange and somewhat disconcerting the first few times I ran a boat in the dark. The rocks, shoals and irregular landforms are no longer visible and easily avoided. On a dark night the boater must rely on memory to know where to go and how to get there. I learned I could improve my night vision if I turned my head sideways and used my peripheral vision, but despite such tricks, it's no secret that distance and depth perception are reduced significantly after dark. To say boating at night gives the novice boater pause would be an understatement.

I recall more than once when Dad said, "Go slow at night! Too many things can go wrong if you go fast after dark. You might miscalculate where the rocks and buoys are, and some boaters ignore the laws mandating the use of running lights. Even if you do everything right there is still the possibility of floating debris that you can't see in the dark."

Most of the time we traveled to a restaurant for dinner or to some other meeting spot to see friends. The TI Club had staff parties in the Golf House on Tuesday nights and A Summer Place bar was another active venue for getting together with friends. There were numerous eating destinations around the river including the Ship and Cavallario's in Alexandria Bay, Heffernan's on Grenadier Island, The Clipper in Clayton, Foxy's in Fishers Landing and the TI Club on Wellesley Island.

Once in a while, I took a date to Gananoque for dinner and the theatre. This trip was about fifteen miles each way and a series of shoal-infested waters along the route made it a tricky outing. Dinner at Heffernan's was also a longer trek. The twenty-mile tour around Wellesley Island became a frequent event on balmy nights when there was a full moon. I remember saying, "What do you think? Should we circumnavigate?"

Sometimes we got together at the homes of our friends at various River locations. I became comfortable traveling five to ten miles up river or down. In the narrow, rocky channels, I'd slow down even more to assure I didn't miscalculate. Hitting a rock at idle speed does far less damage than clobbering it going full tilt.

By the time I was eighteen, I was as confident running a boat at night as I was driving a car. This was during the days before overbearing police scrutiny existed on both sides of the border. Now, in the second decade of the twenty-first century, eleven different species of police roam the river looking to harass the boater too often on the pretext of "homeland security" or a "safety check." Personal freedoms and taking responsibility for one's actions have increasingly become areas that governments think they should control for the good of the individual. The world is ever evolving, and some think it is not improving.

⁒

CHAPTER 38

The Great Blue Heron Adventure

THE RANGE OF boating adventures I've experienced in the 1000 Islands is considerable. I recall one outing that continues to stand out, and I revisit it now as I fondly remember the captain of that occasion, William E. Browning III, who passed away in 2013.

A small contingent of river rats including Browning and myself were enjoying an evening libation at the St James Hotel & Saloon when Bill said, "Tad, I have a group of bird watchers coming from Watertown tomorrow to see what will soon be the Ironsides Bird Sanctuary. I own this island and I'm going to gift it to the Nature Conservancy. Will you row my guests to shore in your skiff, *Bobby,* if I come get you in the morning?"

Libation being the enemy of reason, I said, "Yes."

At ten the next morning on August 31, 1965 up the inside channel between Wauwinet and Cuba Islands came the *Canadian* with Bill at the helm, and along with him an entourage of bird watchers, who were preoccupied leafing through their Audubon manuals and polishing the lenses of their binoculars.

Bill's 42-foot Matthews cruiser was a classic of that wooden-cruiser period sporting a covered aft deck and a roomy main salon where the helm was located. In the bow was a well-appointed galley, a head, a table for dining or sleeping, and more bunks further forward.

His nephew, Marc Aylesworth, had joined the party and he hooked the towrope to *Bobby,* and off we motored down the main channel six miles to Ironsides Island. This island marks the entrance to Chippewa Bay and a collection of the most treacherous shoals in the 1000 Islands. We threaded our way between rocks to the protected side of the island away from the main shipping channel. We identified a convenient area to go ashore and anchored the *Canadian* nearby.

Memory doesn't serve me too well nearly fifty years after the fact, but I recollect Marc and about half a dozen bird enthusiasts went ashore. A Watertown couple was the only members of the group I knew beforehand since they socialized with my parents. The husband was around seventy years old and a keen bird watcher. He relished the idea of clamoring through some thirty acres of underbrush covered with the excrement from hundreds of Great Blue Herons for a close-up look, at what he hoped, would be at least one of these prehistoric looking creatures. His wife's love of these magnificent birds fell short of what he felt, and she opted to stay on board with Bill and me.

While we waited for the bird safari to complete their tour, Bill suggested a spot of coffee, and he said, "Tad come to the galley with me, and we'll brew coffee for the three of us."

The way he hummed and perked up, I knew something was afoot. Sure enough, sequestered in a cupboard was a bottle of Canadian Whiskey. He poured a liberal dollop or two into our two cups while serving our guest an untainted portion of straight coffee.

The three of us sat and mused about the fine outing, and how great it was to protect all these rare herons, which increased our thirst. Before we knew it, a third cup of fancy coffee had come and gone. Here we were talking to the shining star of the "north country," and while I remember little of her appearance and surely regal good-looks, I do recall her dabbing the sides of her mouth with a laced hanky about the time I was scheduled to return for our intrepid explorers. As I prepared to sally forth, our sweet pillar of Watertown society had the oddest change in character. Out of the mouth of this refined lady, cascaded a recitation of off-color limericks each one more bawdy and clever than the one before. "There once was a woman from Nantucket …" Bill's jaw and mine too dropped in unison. I scrambled into the *Bobby* and headed to shore as though I was practicing for the Henley Rowing Regatta. I fetched Marc and one birdwatcher then Marc took over and rowed the remaining ornithologists back to the *Canadian*.

Apparently our bard exhausted her ready supply of limericks by the time our happy band of adventurers returned because the event proceeded without further incident. Bill gifted Ironsides to the Nature Conservancy in 1967, and his many other important contributions to the 1000 Islands are well documented. As the decades passed, I would see Bill at one function or another, and we would revisit the story of our bird watching tour of Ironsides Island. At those rare get-togethers, we mutually agreed that our guest thespian had switched cups with one of us at some point. However, with the passage of time it occurred to me to ask myself, did Bill secrete a dollop or two into our unsuspecting lady's cup simply to spice up the occasion?

CHAPTER 39

⚘

What's My Line?

THE 1000 ISLANDS was a magnet for college age kids when we arrived in the 1960s. A multitude of colleges are located within one-hundred-and-twenty-five miles radius from Alexandria Bay. The local resorts and other businesses needed summer employees to accommodate the tourists and summer residents that flooded the area during the peak season.

The region developed a reputation as a place for young people to go boating, meet the opposite sex, and generally have a blast for a couple of months. My pals and I who were members of the seasonal-resident community shunned the idea of staying near our schools or winter homes in order to get summer employment there. Going to summer school, like my sister Betsy often did, held no interest for me, and the concept of finding an internship for a future career choice had yet to become fashionable. Being at the river for the summer was really all that I cared about.

My parents were inclined to be skeptical of a setting where fun and frivolity is a central theme. The idea that they could be responsible for funding such a program was especially unappealing to them. I discovered that my parents were not alone in their concerns. I've been both witness and the focus of more than one session of parental interrogations with a mom and dad asking questions like, "Where are you going to stay? How are you going to support yourself? Are you mature enough to exercise good judgment in your actions and interactions?" I noticed that the conversations generally moved forward with a repetitive script, "We can't afford to pay for you to waterski, bask in the sun, and party all night. Do you have a confirmed job offer and a legitimate place to live?"

The TI Club, Edgewood, and other local businesses hired dozens of young people as servers, bellhops, bartenders, dock-tenders and other assorted jobs. I preferred a freelance approach.

Clearly a steady flow of interesting characters came to sample the 1000 Islands for one or more summers. Most moved on after a single year while a few became a part of the seasonal landscape. Jim Kiernan was one of those that came and stayed. In the course of patronizing the local saloons, I got to know a wide assortment of personalities. Jim made his mark quickly with his sense of humor and congenial manner. His background was a mystery since he went by the pseudonym of "Jim the Painter" or "Painter" for short. We became friends.

Jim specialized at island painting projects, but he had no boat. I had a boat, and I needed a source of revenue, so I could fund my entertainment expenses that included a special someone and myself. Henceforth, we became partners for the span of that season and the next one too.

Some of the scenes would have made it on a reel of slapstick comedy. I was averse to working on second and third stories so I did the low-to-the-ground painting and Jim did the second and third story work. I remember one project at Little Lehigh Island where we needed to paint the trim on the eves at the top of the building above the second story. One side of the house was perched so close to the water that the ladder was nearly perpendicular to the ground when we leaned it against the structure.

Jim said, "Listen, I see no way to paint the trim on this side of the building."

"I've got a simple solution. I'll hold onto the ladder from the second story windows while you brush on the paint."

"What happens if I fall?"

"That's a foolish question, 'Painter.' You'll get wet, but the good news is you won't get hurt."

Another year Thumper Peach contracted island work that we performed together on other neighboring islands. He was not only a good worker but an even better negotiator. He retired young after putting his talent to work in the corporate world.

Some years, including 1968 and in the early 1970s, I was only at the river for a brief period, and finding a job was unnecessary. In 1968, for example, I arrived at the river after Labor Day just in time for a first class cruise.

CHAPTER 40

⚘

Let's Go Cruisin'

Consuelo and Bobby at dock

DAD LOVED TO collect old things. When I was growing up, we had two Locomobiles, a Chalmers and a 1936 Packard touring car that was our family car. The Chalmers consisted of a wheelbase and an assortment of fenders and other parts scattered around the garage. One of the Locomobiles had been turned into a quasi pickup truck with the back cut out to make space for hauling who knows what. The Packard had no windows and it was necessary to attach side curtains in the case of rainy weather. These cars were relics in the 1950s but Dad loved each one and would only part company if he could add another vehicle of similar age or of more interest to him. He carried on with this tradition after we returned to Comfort Island in the form of his attraction to older boats.

Indeed, we never had a new boat, but Dad bought a small armada of boats that needed engine work and refurbishing but often got neither. As we recognized a need for more boats, he would visit the various marinas and check out what used boats were for sale. A funny old cruiser that he named *Sabot* was added in1964. The name translated means "wooden shoe." There were various theories about the origin of this 32-foot craft and the accepted story is that the boat had spent some years in the New York City area where it had served as a rumrunner among other things. It was apparently built in 1908, which was a fine vintage in Dad's opinion since he was born the same year. The *Sabot* lacked the size and amenities for comfortable overnight cruising, but Mom and Dad nonetheless took it for short one or two-night ventures up the nearby Rideau Canal System.

At the end of the 1967 summer my mom got into the boat-buying act when she purchased a 48-foot, twin-engine Elco cruiser that she and my dad named *Consuelo* meaning "comfort" in Spanish. The new vessel passed muster with my dad since it was built in 1936 and needed work on the engines and the hull. This was a bonafide cruiser with three staterooms, a head and a shower, a galley and a large salon that included the operations center for running the boat. The hull was painted dark blue and the decks were turquoise. The trim and parts of the interior were varnished wood. In short this boat was a stunner in looks and for cruising comfort. My mom bought the boat on credit, and I remember her counting down the payments each month, "Just ten more payments and she'll be ours."

Now that we had a real cruiser, it was time to go cruising. We decided to make the circular trip from Comfort Island down the St Lawrence Seaway to Montreal, up the Ottawa River to Ottawa, down the Rideau Canal to Kingston and back to Comfort Island by way of the St Lawrence River.

Deb kept an informal log of our journey detailing departure and arrival times, and Dad made notations in his diary. The combination of these two resources has provided me with a surprisingly good record of the trip, and it helps me to recall many entertaining events we shared together on our adventure.

At the top of one of the log sheets Deb created her personalized passenger list:

a. Helmsman : Dad
b. 1st Mate / Assistant Helmsman : Tad
c. 2nd Mate / Cook : Deb
d. Cabin Maid / Aft Deck Tender : Mom
e. Food Disposal & Moral Support : "Topper"

The idea of "aft deck tender" gets my vote for one of the funniest things I have ever stumbled across in reading through the family archives. The *Consuelo* aft deck was as cruising-friendly as the rest of the vessel. There were doors exiting the salon on both the port and starboard side that accessed a walkway around the salon and sleeping quarters. The gunwale was raised a foot or more from the deck and chromed posts supported a varnished wooden rail eighteen inches above that. The railing had a hinged section on each side that lifted up so passengers could step off the boat onto a dock. The railing configuration provided safe passage to the bow or stern of the boat even in rough weather.

There was a table attached to the cabin wall that was hinged and folded down parallel to the wall when not in use. We brought several comfortable folding-chairs on board when we were cruising. The arm-rests were varnished and royal blue cushions were removable.

Dad and I took turns piloting the boat, and most of the time it was a simple matter to follow channel markers that defined our route. During those periods when my services were not needed, I pitched-in to lighten the arduous load Mom had been saddled with tending the aft deck. I felt proud to educate myself by consulting a navigation manual titled *Far from the Madding Crowd* written by a Mr. Thomas Hardy.

Like most of our dogs that have become indoor companions, Topper wagged his tail and wiggled underfoot long enough to demonstrate how glad he was to be included in the outing. Nonetheless, having a dog along made life a little more complicated since Topper lacked the ability to use the "head." The weather was also unsociable for some of our journey, which makes taking the dog for a walk a rather unpleasant chore.

Dad never did become a morning person, which was a source of great frustration to my mother, and, indeed, all of us when we wanted to do something before the morning had come and gone. It was no surprise that we didn't get underway until the afternoon of September 9, 1968. We took on water and ninety-two gallons of fuel at Hutchinson's Boat Works. We bore the extra levy that marina's charge with a shrug as we paid the $36 bill.

We motored down the river past the many wooded islands, wetlands and summer dwellings along the route. Gradually the river narrowed as we left the 1000 Islands and made our way toward the Seaway Locks that provide alternative passage for pleasure boats and ships that have no other way to navigate the rapids that keep the water that comes from the Great Lakes moving toward the Atlantic Ocean over this steeper terrain.

Five hours after leaving the marina in Alexandria Bay we had cleared Canadian Customs and were at the Chrysler Park Marina in Morrisburg, Ontario. Deb cooked and we ate on board the first night. The mention in Dad's diary of the "starboard engine stalling off and on" comes under my personal heading of "selective forgetting." I now recollect that I questioned whether the good ship, *Consuelo*, would run the entire ten days necessary to complete the journey.

A mechanic was summoned on day two. He replaced the coil on the starboard engine and the filters on both engines. Most folks would have done all possible routine maintenance before a trip of this length began, but Dad preferred a fix-it as-you-go approach.

We were now two-for-two on afternoon starts with Dad at the helm. Most boaters like to get on the water early then stop early. I advocate this plan myself because if unexpected delays or other obstacles intervene then reaching the night's destination is generally not the cause of acutely elevated blood pressure. Not only that but it allows time to look around the locale to see the sights while observing what might be in the offing for shopping or dining.

We had the first two of the four main Seaway locks a little more than an hour ahead. The Eisenhower and Snell Locks were built to move 700-foot freighters around the initial set of rapids. Pleasure boats move through the locks on a timetable that is in concert with ships going to or from the Great Lakes. It took an hour-and-a-quarter to get through Eisenhower Lock and only thirty-five minutes to clear Snell Lock.

Waiting to lock-through each of the four locks was an opportunity to look around and appreciate the sights. The first thing I noticed was that this was not the entrance to Yosemite or some other scenic wonder. The setting conjures a memory of standing on the runway of a rural airport. There is a control tower that looks like it was built with cement in the 1930s and is the color of sandstone. Wire fences surround the perimeter and viewing areas. The backdrop is not designed with the family in mind, and scanning the complex I sensed that this is what an industrial construction depot looks like.

It was impressive to see a 700-foot ship up close, and watching how a lock raises or lowers a freighter of this size caused me to marvel at this engineering masterpiece.

Going through the locks at Massena slowed our progress and by the time we reached the point where we needed to head off the seaway through a tricky maze of islands, rocks and buoys to our night's mooring, it was dark and we were in the midst of a persistent thunderstorm. I was piloting because I could see better than Dad, and I had the gift of a good sense of direction.

I have a very healthy respect for lightning, and I avoid it whenever possible on the water. Dad stood next to me studying a chart for the location of markers and obstacles. The lightning was actually of assistance because it made it easier to get a bearing as landmarks became briefly visible. However, when a lightening strike was scary-close, I cringed and I ducked my head fearing this might be the "end" for all of us. The strain on my eyes began affecting my mind and visions of being barbecued at sea added a gruesome quality to my stress.

It was after eight o'clock when we reached the Isle Raymond marina. Aside from Topper who never let much of anything bother him, the rest of us were greatly relieved to reach land. We arrived wet and nervous, and I recall breathing a huge sigh of relief. We were rewarded for our effort when we found a club to have, what Dad recorded as, "a fine dinner and drinks."

CHAPTER 41

Leg Two of the Grand Tour: Beauharnois Locks, Montreal & the Ottawa River

RAIN AND WINDY conditions were setting us up to savor the good weather when and if it came. In keeping with Dad's why-start-early program, we made it three-for-three on afternoon starts. We had another pair of locks at Beauharnois. Like the Eisenhower Locks, this is another austere setting with towers and high voltage wires adding to the forbidding atmosphere. It took us more than three hours to get back on our way after waiting for a tanker to come through in the opposite direction. We shared the second lock with a lightly loaded ship named *Christine*. It was like having a pointed four-story, floating college dormitory behind us. When we left the lock the ship passed us like they were the pleasure boat and we were the freighter. I recall Deb saying, "Grab the loose dishes. We're going to get pitched around." A ship of that size throws an enormous wake when going faster than ten-to-twelve knots.

We reached Montreal at 7:30 that evening and secured dockage at the Royal St Lawrence Yacht Club. We took a cab to dinner at the Airport Hilton. I have very little recollection of that stop or the setting. It did, however, mark the completion of the first leg of our four-leg journey.

Dad was continuing to man the helm as we ran our afternoon-start streak to four in a row. Among the nice features of getting on the water early is that conditions are often calmer and more boating-friendly early in the day. As the day progresses winds frequently pick up and the seas grow rougher. This was exactly the case this day as we crossed Lake St Louis in rough seas accompanied by high winds.

We had added gas and water at the Montreal stop, and I see from Deb's log entry that we stopped at St-Anne-de-Bellevue after crossing Lake St Louis. There is a canal and a lock located at this town at the tip of the Island of Montreal between Lake St Louis and Lake of Two Mountains. Boat parking along the canal is abundant with grassy areas, trees and picnic tables located on both sides. The shopping district is adjacent to the north side of the canal. Dad and Deb went ashore and into what Dad described as a "cute French town" with stone and brick buildings huddled close together. Bright-colored awnings added character to the setting. The mission of this trip was to purchase charts for the Ottawa River and to restock provisions for eating on board.

I recall staying with Mom and soon both Topper and I became restless. I consulted Mom saying something like, "Topper needs a walk and I do too. Would you like to join us for a stroll?"

"I'll wait here and read some of my book. I'm getting more than enough fresh air just being on this boat."

Mom was in her mid-fifties, but she lacked vitality. Her inclination to drink to excess once cocktail hour rolled around at five o'clock had negatively affected her health with the passage of time. Mom had been a good athlete and proficient tennis player into her mid-forties, but drinking became an issue she never fully resolved.

We began our trek up the Ottawa River with the knowledge that the boating held a new danger on this leg of the journey. "Deadheads" or short sections of trees that were left behind during various logging operations sank below the surface over time. Without warning some of these logs bob up from the bottom perpendicular to the surface. They were very hard to see and often the first notice of their presence was a thud informing us that this unwelcome visitor had taken a whack at the bottom of the boat. We had several such intrusions before we exited the Ottawa River and luckily none of them connected with our props or we could have been in for a lengthy delay waiting for repairs. When it started to get dark, we headed to port immediately since the deadhead danger multiplied exponentially with no way to see them in advance.

At the end of day four Deb and I devised a plan to jumpstart the boating day. I remember her saying something like, "We've got to get going earlier in the day or it'll be Christmas before we ever get back to Comfort. Let's tell Dad we'll get underway mid-morning and he can join us when he pleases."

"Capital idea." I said.

I had lots of experience running the *Consuelo* and many other boats. Dad agreed that we might be able to make a little better progress by starting earlier. Consulting the charts, it appeared possible to make it to Ottawa the following day where the deadheads and the second leg of the excursion would be behind us. Dad could putter around and get up to speed as he pleased with this new program. Deb's log confirms that we pulled out of Martha's Cove at 8:45 the next morning.

We had one river friend known for his great bravado say to Dad the night before we left on this journey, "Now Mancel I want you to stop at the very exclusive Seigniory Club and tell them Bill sent you. Enjoy the experience."

Well we did stop mid-day hoping to eat lunch there. "Bill who? I'm sorry but he's not in our member directory." Fortunately we brought along *"Consuelo."* I always felt we received a little better treatment at the places we stopped with the *Consuelo* because she was an elegant boat and like a classy lady, people often go out of their way to be accommodative.

We made it to Ottawa at seven that evening. We tied up at the Skiff Club dock adjacent to the northern terminus of the Rideau Canal Waterway. The first eight locks climbed like stairs to the level of the city, but we were too late to lock through that day and too tired as well.

Dad, Deb and I hiked up the steep hill to the venerable old hotel, Chateau Laurier, to be sure it was okay to dock for the night where we had tied up. We also made dinner reservations at Madame Burger's across the Ottawa River in the town named Hull that has since been renamed

Gatineau. A cab drove down to the *Consuelo* and took us to dinner. We stopped into the Chateau Laurier for a nightcap before retiring to the boat for some much needed sleep.

CHAPTER 42

———— ❧ ————

The Rideau Canal Leg of the Grand Tour

THE GOOD WEATHER we had been waiting to savor greeted us the following morning. We began the lengthy process of working our way through the forty-seven locks that transport a boater from Ottawa to Kingston, Ontario where Lake Ontario flows into the St Lawrence River. The Rideau Canal system is a popular cruising destination through a stretch of Canadian wilderness that exhibits incredible landscapes and amazing ingenuity.

Following the War of 1812, the British were seeking a way to connect Upper and Lower Canada without the risk of encountering American forces on the St Lawrence River. The Duke of Wellington, who gained permanent fame defeating Napoleon at Waterloo, advocated building what was to become the Rideau Canal Waterway. Between 1826 -1832 a construction force led by Colonel John By built a series of forty-seven locks and fifty-two dams in addition to digging channels to connect rivers and lakes. The end product was a 125-mile artery of water that connects Kingston, Lower Canada, to Ottawa, Upper Canada. The Rideau Canal Waterway passes through a series of scenic lakes, channels and locks along its route. The canal system is a marvel of engineering and ingenuity.

Much of the work was accomplished with pick, shovel and wheelbarrow. Stones for the locks often had to be quarried miles away and then transported during winter by farmers utilizing sleds and oxen. Gates for the locks were constructed at the lock sites by blacksmiths and carpenters. Simple mechanical tools like lifting cranes assisted by horses or oxen were used to move stones and gates into place. A single gate might weigh as much as five tons.

Most all of the locks are operated by hand even today. A boat enters the enclosure that is 134-feet long and 33-feet wide. The gate is closed and water is then released through an underwater channel to lower a boat or introduced to the lock to raise the vessel. The lock-tender cottages are mainly a collection of quaint board-and-batten structures where the workers stayed before roads and cars made commuting an easy alternative. Well-kept lawns and picnic facilities offer a pleasant contrast to the ascetic settings of the Seaway Locks at Massena and Beauharnois.

Dad and I took turns easing Consuelo into each succeeding lock while Deb and Mom tended the bow and stern lines. Each side of the locks has rubber-covered cables that hang loosely from the top to the bottom of the enclosure. They are bolted to the stones at each end and spaced four or five feet apart. The boater keeps their vessel in place while the lock raises or lowers the craft by looping the bow and stern lines around these cables and holding them in place. Mom became an active participant in our boating team with her responsibility to tend the stern line.

A series of red and green buoys mark the route between Ottawa and Kingston. An oddity of the Rideau Canal Waterway is that the route climbs for over eighty miles to the Rideau Lakes region and then descends for nearly forty miles down to Lake Ontario. In following the channel markers, the rule of thumb is "red right returning." What this means is that in leaving Ottawa the red buoys are on the right because the boat is traveling away from the ocean.

Dad had learned about advanced navigation by taking the Power Squadron Boating course and he pointed out an interesting change to Deb and me, "Did you notice when the route started to descend after Newboro, that the red markers are now on the left rather than the right?

"How come?" I asked.

"It's because we're now traveling in the direction of the ocean rather than away from it, as we were up till Newboro."

We worked our way through sixteen locks on our first day before stopping for the night at the Carleton Golf and Yacht Club near Manotick,

Ontario. We noticed right away that the Rideau Waterway was a mecca for recreational boating in contrast to the Seaway and the Ottawa River. Marinas are plentiful and there are a myriad of lakes and other navigable water along the Rideau route.

Fiberglass was gaining in popularity at the time of our excursion. Most of the boats we saw were used for fishing, touring or water-skiing. An assortment of cruisers also moved either north or south often in unison since the locks tended to define the progress a boat could comfortably advance in the course of a day.

There were many varieties of wooden boats too. Cruisers made by Chris-Craft, Richardson and Mathews were all popular at that time. We saw numerous examples of newer cruisers utilizing a second elevated operating cubicle called a flying bridge. The *Consuelo* could only be operated from a forward position in the salon, but the visibility was good with large windows facing the bow and numerous windows throughout the salon that provided views to the side and behind us.

We made our way through another fifteen locks on the second day including those located at the artistically oriented town of Merrickville that boasts many Victorian buildings and a number of formal gardens. We stopped for our second night below Smiths Falls. While Merrickville was upscale, I recall Smiths Falls as being a "blue collar" community.

There were several manufacturing facilities in the town including the Hershey factory. Getting to town at seven in the evening was after the visitor center closed. Dad, Deb and I walked into town to eat at Top's Marina. Every building we passed smelled like fresh chocolate. A light breeze wafted the aroma of "Chocolate Kisses" my way, and the realization that I was missing the opportunity to buy a suitcase-sized supply of "Reese's Peanut Butter Cups" was reason to sulk for the remainder of our stay. Mom stayed on the boat with Topper unaware of our timing catastrophe.

Deb and I engineered another morning start, and we were cruising through the Rideau Lakes region by the time the coveted "Chocolate Shoppe" opened for business the next day. Topper usually came and sat next to me as I piloted the boat looking to have his ears scratched, but not this day as he could sense my sour disposition.

We had learned our lesson about the consequences of stopping late in the day, and as a novelty, we made it to Chaffey's Locks and the Opinicon Resort at three in the afternoon. Al Cross owned and managed the property, and he was a first class host. He greeted us saying, "Nice to see you again Mr. Clark. I see you brought your own bedrooms for this stay."

We were well acquainted with the venue because we had visited by car and boat on previous occasions. It was a two-day boat trip from Comfort Island via Kingston and only an hour or two by car.

Opinicon consisted of a large central lodge and a number of cabins surrounding the lodge. A sumptuous veranda with brightly painted red chairs and rockers faced a sprawling lawn and a series of lakes receding into the horizon. They had a tennis court, a pool and shuffleboard. Their general store served sandwiches, ice cream and other light dining options. I found a note in Dad's diary saying we had a snack upon arrival.

In front of the general store was a long bench with a five-foot wide sign hanging above the back that amuses me every time I think of it. Two hands stretch in opposite directions and a fish is painted in the middle. On one side of the fish is the word "Liars'" and on the other side is "Bench."

We tied up at the dock for the night. Only twelve locks remained after this day of clearing another four locks. Deb and I swam, played shuffleboard and hit a few tennis balls. We all had dinner together in the hotel dining room. Topper gave such a wag that he wiggled all over when we returned to the boat with a "doggie bag." It seems that dogs never hold a grudge after they have been left behind for a few hours. They are simply happy that someone from the family has returned.

We had logged eight days and nights of what seemed all but certain to be a ten-day cruise. One more night and two more days would complete our journey. We did have an unforeseen burden to deal with when our "stern line tender" was taken ill during the night at Opinicon. Mom was sick all day, which is never fun on a day when the boating weather is nearly perfect. Dad was up early and ready to pilot us through the day's locks, and I reluctantly accepted the formidable task of tending the stern line. Dad, Deb and I had breakfast at Opinicon and lunch at Kenny Hotel at Jones Falls, while Mom stayed on the boat keeping Topper company.

We knew we were getting close to home when the Cavallarios came through Washburn Lock going the other way. They owned a restaurant by the same name in Alexandria Bay that was one of our favorite eating spots.

We cruised thirty miles and went through eight locks before the lock-tenders finished for the day. We were at upper Kingston Mills, which along with Old Slye's is one of the two locations where trains actually pass over the top of the locks. A road also passes by and Dad reported in his diary that a few members of the public stopped to ask questions and share a visit.

Deb showed her creative talents by preparing another tasty meal on board. Our dining choices were limited by the outdated galley, but Deb produced dishes like corned beef hash with egg on top or "Joe's Special" that combined egg, spinach and hamburger into concoctions we enjoyed at home or on board.

Dad seemed to be gaining strength, and he was showing promise in his more active lifestyle whereas Mom was beginning to flag. He piloted the *Consuelo* through the final four locks beginning at 9:00 AM the next morning. This was two days in a row of being at the helm in the shank of the morning. Suddenly Dad was compiling a morning-start streak that might have gone on to equal or surpass his streak of afternoon starts if the cruise had lasted a few more days.

Once we cleared the Rideau Waterway, Dad turned the helm over to me for the forty-mile jaunt home. After many outings focused on learning different regions of the 1000 Islands, I knew a variety of ways to get back to Comfort Island from the Rideau. We motored down the Bateau Channel past the Trident Yacht Club. Sailing was as popular as power boating in this area where the river widened and offered favorable conditions. In fact most of the boats moored at the yacht club were sailboats. Kingston was to become the venue for the sailing facet of the 1976 Olympics.

I guided our return through the quiet passages between shoals and islands fronting several waterfront restaurants, four or five marinas and numerous cottages that constitute Ivy Lea. After dodging lightening bolts on the way to Isle Raymond and "deadheads" on the Ottawa River, I yawned as the *Consuelo* motored serenely through an area that the uninitiated regard as treacherous.

On our approach to the Comfort Island dock, I noticed several members of Mom's afternoon "discussion group" that had seen us coming and were waiting to help celebrate our return. Our landing was like it was following a script. The clock was striking five, and while Topper went to check for any new smells, the rest of us stayed on board to recount the adventure in the company of a refreshing libation.

CHAPTER 43

ᑫ

Notable Canine Characters

PEOPLE ARE NOT the only ones that have enjoyed lazing carefree in the sun on Comfort Island. Topper and other celebrated dogs have been frequent and often long-term visitors in addition to the Clark family members.

Just about every dog that has come to Comfort Island even for a brief visit has become acquainted with the beach. The beach offers a spot where a dog can wade in for a drink, advance a little further to cool off on a hot day or take a swim with a safe place to get out afterwards. I have never heard of or seen a dog try to swim to shore or another island because the distance is considerable and the current is strong near the island with the exception of the area fronting the beach. The younger pooches unabashedly frolic on the large lawns and thrive on being allowed to run loose. There is no dogcatcher on Comfort Island and leash laws don't apply.

It takes a bit of training to convince a new arrival that chasing ducks is a dangerous folly. We watch closely to be sure a novice avoids falling in the river in places where it is hard to get out, and sometimes it is an instructive experience if they do fall in and sample their predicament before being pulled out and returned to safety. So far we have had many dogs enjoy the venue without any tragedies.

We've only had one neighbor throughout most of the years, and there is a considerable buffer between the two main houses on the four-acre island. Their dogs and our dogs have never become a nuisance.

The first dog was Cap Thomson's "rent-a-dog" dating back to the 1880s. I met Cap Thomson in his mid-eighties. He boasted, seventy years after the fact, about renting his dog to Great Grandfather Clark. Cap demonstrated the value of industry, diligence and just plain hard work. Unlike many bits of lore that have trickled down to me regarding Comfort Island history, I never heard any stories about the traits and peculiarities of Cap's "rent-a-dog."

"Jack" was another famous Island dog. He would back slowly down the rowboat slide to give pesky fleas time to scramble up his back onto his neck. He'd wait patiently as the critters made their way onto his head and finally onto his nose whereupon he would dunk his head underwater to unload his unwelcome passengers. He devised this clever way of ridding himself of fleas before the advent of powders, sprays and pills. He was a brown-colored Water Spaniel with fur that was so curly that people thought he had just returned from the beauty parlor after getting a "permanent."

He was known to jump off the dock and swim after departing boats in hopes of getting a ride. And many rides he did get particularly with my great uncle Alson Clark of impressionist-painting fame. We have photos of Alson and Jack pulling away from the dock in the 15-foot sailboat, *Mabel*, with Jack looking both confident and content standing on the bow deck where he was vulnerable to being pitched into the water if the boat swerved suddenly.

I recall Dad reporting that Alson took Jack along on some lengthy sailing excursions to the more open, sailing-friendly expanses near Gananoque, Ontario. The round-trip might entail forty miles or more of sailing. Alson carried a small alcohol stove with him to heat coffee and soup along the way.

"Topper," who joined us on our 1968 *Consuelo* cruise, showed up in 1966, and he made my list of most memorable pooches too. He liked to lie around and sleep most of the time. If he awoke and had to pee, any convenient curtain or piano leg was as good or better than a tree or fire hydrant outside. I remember Topper as an oversized floppy, tan-colored Cocker Spaniel with loose skin. He was as lazy as any two-legged character Steinbeck ever detailed in *Cannery Row*.

Going for a ride in Dad's car or boat, with Dad, was the height of excitement for Topper. He liked to stick his head out into breeze as the boat or car gained speed. I can see his ears now and the way they rose and stretched out on each side of his head until they resembled the wings of an airplane. Topper accompanied Dad almost everywhere. Their personalities meshed perfectly. Neither was in any hurry to get anywhere. Dad gave this critter more mention in his diaries than some family members.

In 1969 I assumed responsibility for my first dog. Dad had named him "Clovelly Chalice" for the purposes of American Kennel Club registration, but he was simply "Hal" to me. He was a sable-and-white Collie, and a member of a litter Dad had raised. Unlike Topper, who mostly liked to loll around and sleep, Hal's most cherished moments were when I'd say, "Do you want to go for a walk?" I'd take him for a walk several times on most days and the way he jumped to attention, wagged his tailed and bowed was evidence of how much he enjoyed this routine.

When I went to the tennis courts or perhaps an even a less productive venue, Hal was prepared to carry-on with his own schedule of orderly behavior. When we were away from home or on the road, I could roll-down the passenger side window and Hal would go out to assess the neighborhood and make new friends. He had a sixth sense about when to head back to the car. He'd jump back through the open window and rest up for his next outing. From my perspective he was quite a dog. It was during that irresponsible period of my life, which some people say never ended. It was a stretch of time when my list of daily chores and obligations sometimes got lost.

Hal closely resembled "Lassie" of television fame. I recall little kids whispering to one another saying things like, "That's Lassie." He was a devoted companion throughout the 1970s and early 1980s. As I look back on it now, I probably doted on Hal as much as Dad doted on Topper. I often told Hal in a tone befitting royalty, "You are some dog."

I knew Hal had reached the gates of the "happy hunting ground" when he became so arthritic that he ceased relishing his daily walks, and so it was that he passed away at thirteen.

CHAPTER 44

Romance

FROM 1961 THROUGH 1965 I spent the school year sequestered seven miles from the nearest town with two hundred boys and no girls. It was not an environment conducive to developing relaxed everyday relationships with the opposite sex. Hebron, Maine and Santa Barbara, California are about as far apart as two places in the contiguous United States can be. My family and friends were in Santa Barbara, which left me indisputably marooned for most of the year.

I know many individuals look back on their high school years as one of the happiest and most stimulating periods of their lives; I look back on these four years with a sense of loss and dread. I can take solace in the fact that I finished the job and graduated, but it was surely more about enduring my high school years than enjoying the high school experience. Summer vacation was like a furlough from prison during this span, and it caused me to appreciate the river more than I might have otherwise.

Even at the age of fourteen when I made my first visit to Comfort Island, I had more than a passing interest in girls. From that 1961 summer to the present, I've held an opinion that the river attracts an abundance of smart and attractive women. I sensed a magical quality to the 1000 Islands the first summer I spent there. It is simply one of those spots that are so beautiful and special that it takes on an added dimension.

I'm not much good at glad-handing and I'll never make it as a politician, but I did develop a boldness when it came to meeting attractive girls. A girl sunbathing on her family dock was an invitation to stop and introduce myself during those carefree teenage summers. "My name is Tad. Do you like to waterski?" The spiel varied but the intent was the same; to meet new and interesting girls, and if they were pretty too, so much the better.

I had a different routine for meeting girls in bars, and it all resulted in making a large number of friends and sometimes lovers from different parts of the river. These were the days when the drinking age was still eighteen and that made for more young people frequenting the local bars. The drinking age in Canada was older than New York so the area got an added influx of Canadians as well. Indeed the bar business was thriving. The law enforcement group was not overly punitive in those days unless a person was doing something utterly foolish. It was party time in the 1000 Islands.

The TI Club was a hub for college age kids that spent the summer at my doorstep. The Tuesday evening staff parties there were legendary for dancing, meeting members of the opposite sex, and guzzling draft beer. Alexandria Bay could be seen from the complex a short distance across the main channel. It was a quick ride there by boat but not many of the summer employees had boats, and the trip by car was much longer and more roundabout. Consequently most of the action stayed contained at the resort and the outlying houses where the help boarded.

In 1966 I became involved in my first serious romance with a girl I met in Santa Barbara named Stephanie Jelacic. We became roommates that spring, and she accompanied me to Comfort Island for the summer. We enjoyed a somewhat solitary summer boating, picnicking and generally exploring the river. I went to college alone in Flagstaff, Arizona that fall, and we gradually grew apart and went our separate ways.

I was still in a mode of adjusting to a world that included both men and women. I had been psychologically scarred during my incarceration at Hebron Academy, and I needed time and space to develop a sense of interacting with society.

When I learned I would not be a participant in the Vietnam War, I moved to San Francisco with a friend and pursued a brief apprenticeship hustling pool for a living. I figured correctly that this would be a fitting venue to learn more about human nature and how to maneuver through the darker recesses of society. I might have learned these lessons during high school, but not while I sat at a desk in a remote corner of the Maine woods. It didn't take long to see that the pool-hustling environment was littered with broken men tagged with nicknames like Fast Eddy, Slim Pickens, Mule and 9-Ball Kelly. They did their best to scratch out a living gambling with anyone who had money to lose. As I studied the game, I realized that even the best tournament players worldwide were unable to make a decent living.

After a year-and-a-half of learning the rudiments of how to play a devious game of pool, I knew tennis was a lot more wholesome sport on every level. Pool is a game that attracts loners and those addicted to gambling, and knew by then that I was neither of those. I liked being in the company of women and nowhere fit that description better than the 1000 Islands during the summer.

My summer romances were not well suited for the long term. One year I had a serious relationship with Sally Gere. Another year it was Anna Hussar then Sandy Sweet and Suzanne Segar after that. Being apart for most of the year, and residing thousands of miles across the country in California provided too much opportunity for growing apart. New acquaintances are made, friendships are formed, and interests develop in divergent directions without the continuity of being together. It is not surprising that long-term friendships are more common in the 1000 Islands than long-term relationships and marriages.

In 1973 I wed Kira Duke. We had a brief romance two years before we became reacquainted. I had won and lost at love often enough by then to know what I wanted for a wife and a long-term companion. My close friend and former college tennis teammate, Stefan Krayk, was our best man, and Kira's sister, Laura, was the maid of honor. We were married at Grenadier Island and followed the ceremony with a reception numbering 200 on the Comfort Island lawn. Our engagement spanned a brief six weeks.

It is one of the ironies of the river that some women come to the 1000 Islands, fall in love with a guy and are smitten with the whole setting while others find no taste for it at all. I was already aware of numerous cases where a guy married a gal from elsewhere, and they moved away for a long time and sometimes forever. I married a fellow river rat and thereby took the guesswork out of the will-she-love-it-here equation.

Kira and I have been lucky enough to share forty summers together in the 1000 Islands since that year when we married. And while some couples do not share a love of the islands initially, I have also seen cases of the dissenting member of the marriage gradually becoming an enthusiastic member of the community as time passes.

Summer and the 1000 Islands are so given to romance that it is no wonder it holds special memories in the hearts of many. A sad reality is that summers end and then most of us young and old alike return to college or distant communities to resume the more responsible aspects of everyday life. A few tears at the moment of departing for another winter is quite common. Each year a bit more of our life is consumed, and one never knows if there will be another year in the magical 1000 Islands to come.

CHAPTER 45

—— ✼ ——

Want to Hit a Few?

MOM AND DAD met on a tennis court in Pasadena, California, and all five members of our family learned to play tennis with some level of proficiency. I began formal instruction in Santa Barbara at the age of ten. I soon caught the tennis bug, and my pals and I would spend our afternoons at the Biltmore courts hitting balls until it was too dark to see. Going to high school in Maine put limits on my expectations of becoming a world-class player, but I have played the game for more than fifty years and I've taught it for over forty years.

Southern California was a hotbed for top-level competitors and some of the best athletes I knew were tennis players rather than football or basketball players. When we began coming to the 1000 Islands in 1961, I brought my tennis rackets with me and looked for people and places to play. I didn't have to look far because the Thousand Islands Club where Mom and Betsy stayed for a month that first summer had a pair of clay tennis courts. The courts I'd played on in California were strictly cement or asphalt, and I'd never even seen a clay court except on television until then.

I've seen old photos of the original TI Club courts with ladies playing in ankle-length dresses and men in white flannel pants. Benches wide enough to seat four were located courtside for spectating. Each bench is shaded by a striped awning overhead. Two such structures had been erected at the side of each court, and there were eight of these sitting areas addressing the four clay courts. A second viewing area behind the East end of the courts consisted of a raised, open pavilion with columns supporting a roof. Spectators watching the matches were in formal attire that included coats and hats for the men and long dresses and bonnets for the women. This is an example of the gilded age of the 1000 Islands around 1890.

By the time I got to the TI Club in 1961, two of the four courts were gone along with most of the benches and all of the awnings. Men now wore shorts and women wore scandalously scant tennis dresses that were so bold as to expose a lady's knees. The pavilion was still there, but it would soon be enclosed to add new hotel units. A small three-sided hut had been built just beyond the sideline of the two remaining courts. This building was used by the tennis pro to store his tennis balls and other equipment. It also provided a shaded seating area for watching the action when people came to play.

Clay courts generally produce a slower bounce and longer rallies. Senior players favor this surface because it is easier on muscles and joints. Effective clay-court playing styles rely less on power and more on consistency. Learning to play well on this surface takes time, practice, and patience.

The other tennis courts in the area were predominantly the hard courts I was familiar with. I was young and impetuous, and I liked the idea of power tennis. It mattered little to me that being two inches shy of six-feet was a handicap relative to developing an overwhelming serve. Furthermore, my groundstrokes were erratic when I attempted to overpower opponents with fast shots from the back of the court. Most points in tennis end because one player or the other makes a mistake. The player who keeps getting the ball back usually takes home the silver platter. The TI Club and Watertown had annual summer tournaments and I'd win a round or two before bowing out to a more consistent opponent.

Members of the river community including John Russell, Trey Vars and Sandy McNally came to play on the clay courts. We had some spirited competitions over the course of my first few summers. John was particularly keen about the game, and he'd call regularly to suggest branching out, "Morning Partner, Estabrook and Parry want to play doubles this

Friday afternoon, I can pick you up and we'll go up to their courts in my boat." Their courts were asphalt courts located in the Thousand Island Park community at the head of Wellesley Island. We developed a fun rivalry with Don Estabrook and Jack Parry that lasted more than twenty years into the 1980s.

TI Park had its inception in 1875 as a Methodist Summer Community under the auspices of Reverend John Dayan who made his name locally as a principle of the revivalist religious movement. The community has the rare designation of being leasehold for all of the cottage owners. Residents do not own their property but lease it. Whereas Comfort Island is an example of Victorian architecture, TI Park is a whole community that embraces this housing theme. Flowerbeds, window boxes, and neat lawns abound. The decorative trim and flourishes found on dozens of these summer dwellings is enough to fill a book focused on examples of Victorian "gingerbread."

There is a central common area with a large playground to one side of an expansive lawn. The field stretches the equivalent of a couple of blocks from the main road to a historic pavilion, docks, and the river. The field serves many purposes from strolling to sitting on a blanket in the sun. Kids play soccer, baseball, football and basketball in various corners of the considerable space. Two tennis courts are located in the Northeast corner next to the road. There has always been a wire fence at each end but no side fences. Two pairs of green wooden benches were placed where the grass met the colored asphalt bordering each court.

John and I played many matches on the hard courts there competing against Don and Jack, and the refreshments afterwards were almost as much fun as the tennis. We cooled down after a hot game of doubles with either "Orange or Raspberry Blossoms." The ingredients were easy to remember. All that was needed was a blender, Vodka and orange or raspberry sherbet.

My high school team won the Maine State Championship my senior year and I played two years of junior college tennis for the Santa

Barbara Community College team. I was beginning to spend more time working on my tennis and less time wondering how soon we could get to the refreshments. I stayed at Comfort Island late into the fall of 1970. John Russell, Dee McElhern and whomever we could get for a fourth would drive a hundred miles to Syracuse and back in order to play indoors after the weather soured. I got to know one of the instructors at the facility named Bob Kulig. He and I played a couple of times, and one day he asked, "Why don't you join me for a tournament trip to Europe next spring. I've written away for tournament schedules, and we could quaff down a few select European beers when we're not on the courts."

Bob had played number-one singles at Colgate University and was an experienced tournament player. This was an opportunity to get a taste of world-class competition, and what I saw changed my view of tennis forever.

We played three professional tournaments. They were all contested on slow European red clay courts. We received appearance money and prize money for each event.

The first event was a mid-level event in Neuchatel, Switzerland. Bob advanced to the later rounds and essentially won a doubles match for us on the strength of his game alone. I was dismissed in short order in my first professional singles match.

The second tournament was an entry-level event in Cannes, France. I learned more about what it takes to win tennis matches in those ninety minutes of competition than I ever learned before or since in such a brief span of time. I remember explicitly the fellow I played. He was short, squat and he certainly did not have an athletic appearance. As we warmed up, I saw examples of stroking technique no one would ever teach or want to learn. When the contest began, my opponent was transformed into a marvel of quickness and agility. I wondered if I was playing one opponent or two because everywhere I hit the ball no matter how hard or how close to the lines the suddenly spry little fellow was there to float it back. The result was never in doubt, and I was on a two-match losing streak.

My third event was in Heerlen, Holland and this was a world-tour level event. Somehow Bob convinced the tournament organizer that I was an "A" player from California that should be included in the draw. Bob must have been more than convincing because when the draw was released, I was the number-five seeded player. I played a college standout from Rice University. He was one of the last players accepted into the event and lost badly in the next round, but he dispatched me 6-1, 6-1. I remember the father of my host family trying to console me by saying, "Just an off day, Tad."

I didn't have the heart to tell him that this was as well as I could ever remember playing up to that point in my development.

I spent the next five years and countless hours working to become an accomplished tennis player and gradually the hard work paid off. When a rally got to fifty shots, I hoped it would reach a hundred. I learned to attack when good opportunities presented themselves and keep the ball in play otherwise. I captured a Southern California open tournament in 1974 and the Championships of Galway, Ireland in 1975. I won many tournaments in the years that followed, but I credit that afternoon in Cannes, France as the catalyst that caused me to appreciate that becoming an adept tennis player was not a gift that was going to arrive in my mailbox one day. I realized that it was going to take focus, hard work, and dedication to bring my tennis-playing aspirations or some other worthy goal to fruition.

CHAPTER 46

❦

Making My Vocation My Vacation

It amazes me how inconsistent the phenomenon of age is. Numerous times I've had a conversation with one of my young tennis students that goes something like this, "How old are you, Hannah?"

"I'm five-and-a-half."

"How about that. You're the same age as Anna."

"Oh no, she's not my age. She just turned five."

For a kid a year is a very long time, but as I approached middle age the years seemed to fly by at an ever-quickening pace. Each of us only has so many years allotted to us before we pass on. I had my first experience with the death of someone close to me in 1971. Mom was diagnosed with cancer while I was in Europe, and she died less than a month after my return. My dad's mother, who lived adjacent to us in Santa Barbara, died a month later. Mom was fifty-eight and hadn't lived either a long or a full life. Grandma was ninety-four and had lived too long. Life is not always fair, which was a lesson I learned and saw repeated more than once.

I graduated with a two-year degree slanted toward English in 1973, and I married Kira later the same year. Dad had moved into his mother's house while Kira, Deb, and I assumed tenancy at the old homestead next door.

Kira's family had a summer cottage on Grenadier Island. This is the same island where Heffernan's Restaurant was located, but their residence was on the west side rather than the east, and at the head of the island rather than the foot. The Duke location had the convenience of being situated closer to the neighboring communities of Rockport, Ontario and Alexandria Bay, New York. The west side of the island faces the Canadian mainland while the east side faces the Seaway. The Grenadier setting was more tranquil and the boating traffic was subdued compared to Comfort Island where activity was teeming on and around the main shipping channel.

Kira's great grandfather, C. A. Duke, purchased the original farmhouse in 1906 from the Root family. The Roots had farmed the parcel back during the period when Grenadier Island was still an agricultural community. At one time there were fourteen farms and over two hundred acres under cultivation. A dirt road ran the six-mile length of the relatively narrow island linking all the properties. A one-room schoolhouse was built then rebuilt twice more between 1818 and 1927. In 1963 the school closed its doors for the final time. Typical of rural one-room schools the building was a site for educating the kids and also the social center of the community. Gradually the farmers moved to shore and most of the land is now overgrown once again with thick underbrush and trees.

In 1973 the cottage was little changed from the days when the Roots lived there. A living room with a fireplace, a kitchen, a bedroom, and the only bathroom in the house were on the first floor. Three more bedrooms were on the second floor.

Kira's Uncle Bud Duke maintained a large two-story boathouse as his residence on the same property. He had a pair of sons named George and Paul that soon became two of our best friends.

The Duke property adjoined the Grenadier Island Country Club, which was founded by a group of families in the area including C. A. Duke who was Kira's great grandfather. The original members adopted a theme of an unpretentious setting and modest facilities. The golf course had no watering system for the fairways and the corridor from tee-to-green consisted of a sandy soil mixed with dirt and occasional tufts of grass. The accepted rule was to hit a shot, and if it wasn't on the green or lying in a rare patch of grass, the player was allowed to place their ball on a nearby tuft and hit their next shot. The clubhouse was a wood-framed building with exposed studs in many sections without insulation. Screens surrounded the dining room and main gathering areas. Rustic was a good basic description of the building and "fancy" was nowhere to be seen.

Kira's father, Charley, and I shared a friendly relationship and had numerous occasions to play golf on the all-but-vacant course together. Club membership was dwindling in 1973 and the survivability of the venue was becoming a serious matter until a few of the remaining members proposed reinstituting tennis to attract a younger generation of new supporters.

I had been teaching tennis in Santa Barbara for two years by the time the courts at Grenadier Island were set to reopen in 1975, and it was a natural fit for them and me. They needed someone to run the operation, give lessons, and greet potential new members, and I needed a summer job with the prospect of revenue and longevity. The club enjoyed a renaissance with the addition of tennis and clearly the fit has worked quite well for us both since my tenure there is approaching forty years, and the club currently has more than one-hundred-and-fifty active members.

Despite the fact that this summer job was three thousand miles removed from the winter site, nonetheless, I now had a year around job. This would not last for long however.

By 1978 Dad had remarried a much younger woman named Natalie Hanson, and he decided it was time to sell the family homestead. I learned firsthand that infatuation is not reserved for only the young and innocent.

I had received an offer to manage the Watertown Racquet Club for the indoor winter season at the same time I was being evicted from the Santa Barbara home where I grew up. Deb was living in the Watertown area already, and she drove west to help clear out the house and to assist us with our move. We stored many of our possessions and brought the rest of them east in the U-Haul that Deb towed.

From the racquet club it was only a half-hour drive to Comfort Island. We were able to commute back and forth whenever the weather was favorable. I liked this arrangement, but this was not destined to last more than the single season. I managed the club for Watertown Savings Bank who took over the business when the owners filed bankruptcy. I put in seventy to eighty hours a week reviving the business, and the club was showing a tidy profit by the time the season ended. Chet and Nancy Gray purchased the property and took over operating it themselves.

My close association with those in the area who had an interest in tennis increased the demand for my teaching services greatly. Several communities including Alexandria Bay and LaFargeville hired me to conduct junior tennis programs. I taught private lessons at several other locations in addition to running weeklong tennis camps at the Grenadier Island CC. My lesson schedule was fully booked. This had the obvious benefit of helping to pay more bills, but there were other rewards too.

Mark Twain counseled his audiences that, "The secret of success is making your vocation your vacation." This quote sums up my love of teaching tennis and for working with kids in particular.

In my childhood and early teens I shared very few outings together with Dad. Mom used to take us to the beach almost every day during the first summers in Santa Barbara in the early 1950s, but after we moved there permanently in 1952, we stopped going as often and eventually not at all. Mom and Dad liked to go out to eat with us once or twice a week, but hitting tennis balls together, going fishing, taking a hike, or attending a professional sporting contest was a rare occurrence. My experience with these activities was usually with a friend or under the direction of a private camp program.

I felt I missed out on something important not having a closer parent-child relationship with Mom and Dad. It helped me to appreciate that it is important for kids to have someone that is receptive to listening to their concerns. I made a point of talking to kids like I would talk to an adult. I treated them as equals, and I had a genuine interest in what was on their mind. Because I treated kids the way I did, I built rapport with them. As they became adults themselves, I didn't have to shift gears and take on a new persona around them. We had already established a line of communication that works at any age.

CHAPTER 47

The Unpaid Help

COMFORT ISLAND WAS designed to operate with a staff. When Great Grandfather Clark and his family came for their first summer in 1883, they brought along a butler, a maid, and a cook. Locally they hired a captain for the steam yacht, an engineer, a caretaker, and laborers as needed.

When Dad married Natalie in 1974, his dedication to Comfort Island declined. Ivan Ford was a retired Adirondack Park Ranger who became a security guard for the Stillwater Hunting Club after that. He took over caretaking duties in 1968 after Ronald Shutler resigned to buy a dairy farm. Ivan did a little mowing and some cleanup, but we generally thought of him as a carbon copy of Dad, who liked to putter around and reflect on the past. They were more like brothers or buddies rather than employer and employee. His role in shouldering a significant share of the upkeep of Comfort Island diminished with each passing year. When Dad died in 1981, Ivan was possibly more relieved than worried about what he would do next for employment.

Ivan was the last paid caretaker at Comfort Island. Kira, Deb and I shared the chores and maintenance for the years that followed. Deb became less involved in island activities as the years passed, and she eventually moved back to California in 2006, and 2007 was the last time she came for a stay.

Kira and I lived close enough to commute for just the one year we managed the racquet club. Most other years we came and stayed for whatever length of time we could allot. By default we assumed the majority of the duties associated with maintaining the grounds and the house.

What the uninitiated don't realize is that island living has a romantic image that doesn't always align with reality.

The Clark property on Comfort Island was approximately two acres, and much of the land was steeply sloped and covered with lawn or scrubs. It was a big job getting the grounds in shape each year.

I developed a technique that assisted me in accomplishing the task. I took on the project in bite-size chunks. First, I'd collect the sticks and branches that the oaks, maples and birch trees shed, and I'd move them to a burn pile or into recesses in the seawall that benefited from what would become dirt and mulch in the future. Next, I would mow a manageable section, rake the trimmings and add the residue to the branch pile. I would repeat this process until the yard was fully cleared and manicured.

Dealing with underbrush consisting mostly of lilacs required constant pruning or they'd take over entire corners of the property after only a year or two. Sometimes I used a chainsaw to cut back the overgrown lilac forests. The terrain was rough on equipment and there is a large collection of crippled mowers under the house. I recall mowing one section of the back hill where the mower was typically at eye level.

Things were no easier in maintaining a 6500 square-foot house. Dogs make good companions, but Deb had dogs and so did we. While derelict mowers cluttered the space under the building, broken vacuum cleaners littered spare closets and obscure hallways inside the house. Kira and I had the vacuum cleaner and mower going in stereo some days.

The music produced in the process of doing island chores is quite a bit different than the Percy Faith theme song for the Hollywood movie *A Summer Place*. The soft refrains of the music score do not mirror the real-life exertion required for island living. The stereotype task of going shopping is more than hopping in the car and off I go.

I would have to clamor into a boat that may be rocking due to wave action or otherwise hard to board because of the level and stability of the dock. Will the boat run? Boats are not like cars or airplanes, and having the boat not start is a common occurrence. Assuming the boat does start I now pilot the craft to shore. Wind, cold and inclement weather are elements that may complicate this step in the process. Finally I hop into the car and go do my shopping. Upon return, it is necessary to carry the supplies some distance to the boat and load them accordingly. Once back to the island dock the supplies are unloaded and placed in a cart that has to be pushed up the steep hill to the awaiting stairway that climbs to the house. But wait, this is not the final step. Refuse and recycling must make a return trip to shore for disposal.

Launching and hauling boats in the boathouse added to the workload. Shutters have to be taken off and stored in the spring then put back on in the fall. It is a big job maintaining an island, and we certainly learned to appreciate how difficult it is to do this work with no outside help.

For career purposes as a photojournalist, Betsy had assumed her given first name and was going by "Ellen" by the time she married Geoffrey Williams at the island in 1980. Dad and Natalie came for the wedding after they had skipped the 1979 summer at Comfort following the bitter disagreement he and I had about his decision to sell the entire Santa Barbara property. I considered it ironic that he had given the home there the nickname of "forsaken acres" during the period from 1950 – 1952 when we left for the winter to be in Pasadena, and how this nickname turned out to be a harbinger of the future.

It was apparent that Dad's health had declined ominously in the intervening year. He never had a regular fitness regimen, and he used to chuckle when he'd report, "I never seem to gain or lose a pound, but when I'm at the island for the summer, I find that I have to take my belt in four or five notches as I repeat the hike up to the house day after day." Back in Santa Barbara Dad would take the car to go get the mail, which was only a two-hundred-foot walk from the front door. He was unsteady walking on this visit, and he had several instances where I had to assist him when he got confused landing the *Buzz*.

He had a stroke during the winter, and I never saw him again. All the years of managing the family finances, and his talk about making preparations for the family's financial future had been a sham. Natalie was the primary benefactor of his estate, and he hadn't even made a provision for us kids to receive Comfort Island, which held no interest for Natalie at all. We were forced to untangle the mess in court. We received the island while Natalie received essentially everything else.

In 1983 we had a centennial party celebrating this hallmark of the Clark occupancy at Comfort Island. A sizable number of Clark relatives came from California, Illinois, Washington DC and other places to attend the event. It was a shame that Dad missed the occasion after all he'd done to keep the legacy alive for so many decades. His cousin, Alce Ann Cole, rented the Papworth boathouse next door to station her large contingent of family and friends connected to the Edwin Clark branch of the family. Scores of our friends from the river and neighboring states attended.

It was an afternoon affair complete with a small band that played mostly background music. The weather was sunny and warm, which seemed fitting for such a special occasion. Bunting adorned the tower railing and bright colored signal flags were attached to the front porch soffits. I remember asking Deb, "Do you think we'll make it to one-hundred-fifty years here?"

She thought for a moment and then said, "Maybe one-hundred-and-twenty-five years is more realistic." I'm here to say we did make it to one-hundred-and-twenty-five and beyond, but one-fifty was proving to be too optimistic.

1983 Centennial celebration

CHAPTER 48

⁌

The Full Catastrophe

By 1984 I was married and had a steady job. We had a home complete with mortgage payments and the only thing missing was a couple of kids. Zorba, in the movie *Zorba the Greek,* presents an amusing slant on the path we were about to follow when he answers the question about whether he has ever been married, "I'm a man, so I married. Wife, children, house, everything...the full catastrophe," but we were happy and excited to welcome our son, Charles Talcott into our lives on September 11, 1985.

Kira and I debated whether we should have more than one child, which was a debate she won easily when she posed the question, "Do you want to be in the entertainment business twenty-four hours a day for the next eighteen years?" Charles was not yet two when Victoria Ashleigh joined our family on June 1, 1987.

It wasn't long before Charles picked up the nickname of "Coty" and Victoria, was also young when she became known as "Tori." They both entered this world at the Watertown Good Samaritan Hospital, which coincidentally had been where Mom passed on from this world. They spent the first weeks and months of their lives at Comfort or Grenadier Island. They were destined to become river rats like their parents.

Kira had been at Grenadier Island during her infancy, and she had a keen awareness for having fun while keeping everyone safe. Ellen-Betsy, Deb and I were all teenagers when we came to Comfort Island for our first summer. We did have an early upbringing that included spending many summer days on Santa Barbara's Miramar Beach, but there was more potential for fun at the river and also more danger.

Young and old alike need to learn to respect the river. Many individuals have perished in the waters of the St Lawrence River. State laws mandate that children must wear life jackets in boats until they reach the age of twelve, but some families don't take precautions around seawalls, docks and boathouses despite the obvious danger. We had both Coty and Tori wear life jackets when they were going anywhere near the water.

A bit of early Comfort Island lore entailed Great Uncle Edwin who fell headfirst into a rain barrel on the boathouse dock in the mid-1880s. He would have certainly drowned if the caretaker, George Root, hadn't heard the commotion and pulled him out feet first.

Comfort Island was a paradise for kids. The beach is outside the front door, the docks and seawall are readymade for fishing, and boating is an everyday occurrence. Taking boat rides was a preferred pastime, and with darkness delayed by daylight savings time and the longer days of June and July, I remember numerous evenings when I'd say, "Anyone up for a boat ride?"

Sometimes the kids and I would take the Mad Hatter and putter nearby, and other times all four of us would take a faster ride up the main channel in the Wellcraft.

Comfort beach with freighter in background

The allure of the beach strikes me as having a strong appeal to almost every kid. As a preschooler in Santa Barbara, I used to build drip castles protected by motes reinforced with seaweed. At the Comfort Island beach Coty and Tori had a potpourri of plastic toys including buckets, shovels, watering cans, action characters, boats, and land vehicles to go along with inflatable devices they rode while in the water.

They would spend hours at a time building and acting out an endless number of pretend scenes at the water's inviting edge. I was witness to the fact that the rest of the world doesn't exist when one is immersed in the adventure and drama of make believe.

CHAPTER 49

❧

Is It a Picnic or a Shore dinner?

Mamie C towing houseboat Comfort up Rideau

HELEN BALFOUR AND her husband, John, were friends with Great Grandmother and Great Grandfather Clark. Their first entry in the Comfort Island guest book is July 18, 1883, which was less than three weeks after my great grandparents arrived that first season. Helen had a passion for painting, and she had a distinct influence on my great uncle Alson becoming an artist. She specialized in watercolors, but we have a mirror that one art collector characterized as, "The finest piece of 'river art' I've ever seen."

The panels surrounding the mirror were painted some time during the mid-1880s. There are four larger scenes on the four sides of the mirror and four smaller squares in the corners. The top panel depicts the family leaving the Comfort Island dock in the steam yacht, *Mamie C*, towing three rowing skiffs on their way to a fishing picnic that is still locally referred to as a "shore dinner." Going clockwise the next large panel shows a member of the party standing in one of the skiffs fishing. The third rectangle details a picnic table complete with white tablecloth and place settings. The final section shows the skiffs and steam yacht from behind as it motors into the sunset. The smaller squares in each corner are vignettes that display a basket of flowers, a pot boiling over a fire, a string of freshly caught fish, and a lady reading in a hammock.

Balfour mirror depicting picnic outing

I was brought up in a breakfast-lunch-dinner family, but I realize that the breakfast-dinner-supper alternative is also popular in many regions worldwide including the 1000 Islands. Folks who do strenuous manual labor like farmers and the early fishing guides, who rowed their customers many miles in St Lawrence Skiffs in the later half of the nineteenth century, had reason to eat a hearty meal at the noon hour. They called it their "dinner," and I'd agree with that definition. Instead of meat and potatoes or fish and starch, I grew up eating a sandwich or a burger. I'd classify my version of the noon repast as "lunch." The "shore dinner" as opposed to a "picnic" is an extension of the dinner versus lunch theme.

The common denominator between a shore dinner and a picnic is that it is an opportunity to explore different scenic areas in a leisurely, relaxed fashion. We began going on picnics with Tori and Coty when they were infants. Kira would load the brown wicker picnic basket into the red Wellcraft outboard, and I often asked, "Should we head downriver to Chippewa Bay or upriver to the Grindstone area today?"

I'd head the boat to whatever destination we had decided to visit that day while touring through intricate channels and clusters of islands for thirty to forty-five minutes before finding a suitable uninhabited spot to tie the boat and go ashore.

One of our favored spots was a stand-alone rock off a point connected to Grindstone Island facing a narrow cut and the Jolly Island shoreline. This was in the vicinity of the Muskellunge spawning grounds and a short distance downriver from the "forty-acres" fishing area that has gained fame for some of the trophy sized "Muskies" that have been caught there. Fish measuring more than four feet in length and weighing more than fifty pounds have been caught here. Yes, they have teeth.

I'd idle the boat into the cattail rushes behind the rock and tie it to a boulder that had a space below it where I could loop the bow line under the rock and then secure it on top. It was then possible to step onto the rock right from the boat.

Lichen decorated the surface of this big boulder like it does on many rocks in the 1000 Islands region including the flagstone walkway at Comfort Island. The areas receiving the most sun were mostly green or gray with the dry wiry growth, while the more shaded sections displayed patches of orange. It can become quite slippery when it is wet.

We'd clamor up the steeper side of the rock before following the gentle contour down the other side. A couple of grassy areas and a few stunted hemlocks and other shade trees made a swell place to sit on our blanket while we ate. It was amazing to me that any vegetation could scratch out an existence on a barren rock like this.

Fishing boats zipped through the cut every so often, and a seven-foot ledge offered the perfect place to jump or dive into the deep water at the edge of the passageway. The downriver end of the rock eased gently into the water and a crevice offered a convenient stairway for climbing out after the swim.

We did almost all of our picnicking at lunchtime, and it was rare to picnic in the evening then idle home with the sunset. Whether it be lunch or dinner, I'd classify these picnics as one of life's great experiences, right up there with having kids.

CHAPTER 50

꩜

A Bump in the Road

IN JUNE OF 1991 Coty and I were passengers in a car operated by Paul Quackenbush who was the father of one of my most promising tennis students. It was a two-hour drive from Alexandria Bay to see his older son, Tony, play his first tournament in Utica. Paul and his wife, Terri, were separated, but she was agreeable to bringing Tony to the site. Paul, Coty and I never arrived. Paul had an undisclosed sugar disorder that caused him to fall asleep after eating. We had a sandwich in Watertown. The car was on cruise control thirty minutes later when he dozed off on a two-lane road near Pulaski. Before I could grab the wheel we had a head-on collision with a three-quarter-ton truck.

It was a miracle that Coty and I lived, but Paul was not so fortunate and he died at the scene. Coty had a closed-head injury, a femur with multiple fractures and the ball joint had been sheared off the hip of his other leg. He spent three days in a coma.

I arrived at the hospital with eight units of blood pooled in my abdomen. Somehow I survived and those I talked to that attended various facets of the emergency surgery marveled at the wizardry Dr. Howard Simon demonstrated in pulling me through. When he discharged me, I asked him how close a call I'd had. He said, "You are the first to walk out of here considering the state of your arrival." I gave silent thanks for all the years of training I'd done to become a top tennis player because this was surely why I survived.

We spent the entire summer and into October convalescing. The doctors would not allow us to stay on Comfort Island that summer, and we would have been physically unable to do so even if we had wanted to. We had to scramble to find places to stay, and it was costly renting during the peak season. Coty, in particular, had a multitude of hospital appointments in Syracuse, and any time he went somewhere Kira had to lift him and his heavy cast into the car.

Coty was only five when the accident occurred but he showed remarkable courage and resilience in the way he handled such adversity. At one stage he wore a cast from his chest to his ankle on the leg with the fractured femur because it wasn't healing properly. While still in the hospital he asked me, "How come this had to happen to me, Dad?"

I answered, "I don't know, Coty, but you will recover from this whereas some of the kids here will never be the same again." Coty never voiced another complaint.

In 1992 we returned to Comfort for the summer. The previous summer had been rough on all of us but particularly Kira. She wanted someone to help with Tori who had just turned five and Coty who was not yet seven. One of our friends, Anna Price, had a girl come from Arizona to help with her kids, and she suggested we do the same with a girl that lived next door to her at their Tubac winter residence. Mireya became an au pair to our kids while I worked and Kira provided for the household. Coty was literally back on his feet, and I was running my tennis programs again.

The 1000 Islands was a great place for raising kids, and I knew many youngsters of all ages because I taught them tennis. When Coty and Tori got to be four or five, they began coming to play tennis too.

We have never had commercial television service on Comfort Island, which Kira and I viewed as a healthy decision since it got our kids outdoors, and it also encouraged them to create their own fun rather than being entertained by frivolous television shows.

Part of our routine included going out to eat with Coty and Tori once a week and then eating out a second time by ourselves. The kids were a credit to themselves and us by virtue of the good behavior they displayed in the restaurant environment. We enjoyed having them along when we dined out, and they loved being there.

I recall an evening when we went to an upscale French restaurant in Lake Placid called La Veranda. We had made a reservation, but I sensed by the way the host scanned the reservation list that he was chagrined to see two small children. Sitting quietly and talking about the events of the day or topics of current interest was typical of a family evening out. As other patrons began to leave, several stopped by our table to compliment the children on their stellar conduct. I remember one lady saying something like, "We kind of wondered what to expect when you walked in, but I think your kids acted a good bit better than some of us."

Having Mireya living with us made it easy and convenient for Kira and I to share an evening by ourselves once a week. Mireya was from Chile, and I'm guessing she was in her mid-twenties in 1992. She came and stayed with us for three summers before she moved on. She spoke broken English and enjoyed playing any number of games with the kids. When it was our turn to go out alone, Mireya and our two kids fantasized about the dining experience in their own special setting. It was a game they called "restaurant." This dining-out game was perhaps the favorite of all the games they played together.

The "Crazy Clarks' Café"

At the head of the table sat the white teddy bear, "Cloud." Next to him sat a favored white monkey named "Snowball," and at the other end sat the gray gorilla with the half-peeled banana. Five seats in all were filled with stuffed animals. The table was a black wooden hope chest with carvings on the sides and top. The initials AMM shared space on the top surface along with the recessed outlines of leaves, branches and a flower at the end of each branch.

Every chair was distinct but they all adhered to a general theme of a caned seat. One of the ten varnished wooden-framed dining table chairs accommodated the gorilla, Cloud was in a wooden Victorian chair painted a fading yellow with the rounded flourishes painted black. Snowball was in the ancient perambulator with wire-spoked wheels, leaf springs, and wooden armrests connected to the metal framing. Several other occupants shared a wooden kid's rocker with spindles adorning the arms and back support.

The table was set with a number of white nondescript coffee cups and an assortment of silver colored vessels including a water pitcher, a chaffing dish, a serving bowl, a teapot and more. They had an order pad that the proprietor of the Chez Paris diner in Alexandria Bay had given them. They used the pad to jot down their customers' orders. Their spelling employed a form of shorthand that mirrored the creative genius of youth and make believe -- "1 bol onin supe."

CHAPTER 51

❦

Mom Called It Her "Mad Room"

EVERYONE NEEDS THEIR space, and another slick feature of Comfort Island is that there is space galore. Kira and I took over the upstairs bedroom facing the main channel after Deb moved to the three-room maid's complex. I took over the room next to ours where Ellen-Betsy stayed during her early years, and I turned that room into what Mom had identified as a "mad room." I never quite figured out what she meant by that, but I do realize it was about having a place to go to get away from it all.

Mom's mad room was situated off the living room that later became known as the catchall "antique room." The room had a large, varnished oak desk with pigeon holes located at the far edge of the writing surface. I remember her stowing things like the *Consuelo* payment coupons, correspondence, and stationary in the handy compartments. She also kept things like knickknacks and other personal items in the drawers. Some of her sizeable hat collection found a temporary home on or next to the desk as well.

Deb had her own office next to her room in the maid's quarters. Kira grew to like the dining porch as her daytime getaway venue. Dad took over the spacious room next to the room with the upstairs fireplace where he and Mom slept.

My special area was a cozy and solitary setting where I could contemplate and create. I received a padded rocking chair for my birthday in the early 1970s that I placed in an optimal position to view the channel and the Narrows. I used this hospitable seat until the armrests had no fabric left and the rocking apparatus broke. I replaced it with a new rocking chair not once but twice.

I had a throw blanket that I'd cover my lap and legs with when the weather was uncivilized. I occasionally used a space heater too when it was cold enough to snow or in several instances when it was snowing. I also had a quaint metal fan that served me well when it was hot and humid. I always thought that someone clever created the suggestive name of "Summer Frost" for that product.

The river view is dynamic even when there are no ships or boats passing. The bottom is more than two hundred feet deep in this section of the river, as a torrent of water tries to squeeze through the Narrows in order to catch up to its liquid kin that is meandering further downstream in the wider expanses. The irregular shapes of the bedrock that anchors the surrounding islands to mother earth spin the rushing fluid every which way. Whirlpools, currents, counter currents and flat calm areas interact like a rhythmic, exotic dancer slowly changing its shape and patterns on the liquid canvas below.

View from second floor office

The room was a wonderful venue where I could depot all my collected treasures. For six decades I stockpiled clothes, shoes, books, papers, artifacts, and close to a thousand golf balls I found at the Grenadier golf course. I had a pair of tables in front of the chairs where I piled notes, correspondence, pens, arrowheads, tennis medals, keys, and just about anything else imaginable until I needed to find something, which became a motivating reason to tidy up.

Tennis has readymade participation in places like southern California and Florida where I taught during the winters, but in northern New York and Canada it is a challenge to entice kids to play and enjoy the sport. I spent many hours in my mad room developing ideas and designing events to make tennis something special and fun for the young people who came to my lessons.

During the winter months I put in extra study to prepare myself to run the best programs possible each summer. It became apparent that a three faceted education would produce the best results. Learning about physical training, teaching methods, and mental disciplines defined my areas of study. I learned from experts like Harry Hopman about training, Vic Braden about teaching strokes, and Tim Gallwey about accessing mental states conducive to peak performance.

I typed my programs, training notes, schoolwork, and correspondence on a 1940 vintage Underwood Typewriter for many years before computers came on the scene around 1990. The computer took the drudgery out of editing my work. I could "cut and paste" to improve a presentation, and if I had grammar errors or spelling mistakes, fixing them was as simple as pressing the delete key and retyping the affected section. The computer undoubtedly improved my writing overnight. I could now think about what I was going to say rather than worrying about how to get the general message onto the paper without mishap.

Having so much free space is a luxury that comes with living in a mansion. The Grenadier house is big but nowhere near the size of Comfort, which is okay when the weather is pleasant because there are an array of seating options on one of the two outside porches. However when it turns cold, and other family members are there to share the limited indoor space, it causes me to long for my mad room at Comfort Island.

CHAPTER 52

⚬

The Joys of Dog Rearing

Woody

AN ACCOUNT OF early notable dogs at Comfort Island has been covered previously, but in 1995 Coty, Tori and Kira mounted a campaign to acquire a family dog. They teamed up against me after an island neighbor began selling a litter of Yellow Labrador puppies. I held out while they sold most of the puppies, but when the owners offered to give us one late in the season, the pro-dog crusade picked up steam with all the classic rhetoric, "Please Daddy, pretty please. We'll take care of it. We'll feed it and take it for walks. We'll brush him and give him baths. You'll see you won't have to do a thing."

The team was relentless and finally I said, "Okay." Because I'd made and broken the same promises when I was a kid, I had no doubt that it wouldn't be long before the responsibilities would be Kira's and mine.

Unfortunately, I never had a chance to see if my children would live up to their promises because our new dog had ingested some twine before we owned him, and a few weeks later we were forced to put little "Sunny" to sleep. It was a very sad experience for the whole family, and we were all in agreement that we'd have to replace Sunny with one of his relatives.

We contacted the appropriate breeder in Wisconsin, and several weeks later "Woody" arrived at the Asheville air terminal where I picked him up. He was only eight weeks old and groggy from being sedated for the flight when I aired him on the grass adjacent to the terminal. I thought to myself, "What a calm and mellow puppy." I have seldom been more wrong in my initial assessment of any critter before or since.

It turned out that we had just become the dumbfounded owners of the most energetic dog I ever owned. I theorized that he could run the Iditarod Dogsled Race all by himself without the usual fifteen teammates to help pull.

We called him "Woody, the wonder dog" because we wondered why we got him. Woody wasn't mean and he didn't bite, he was simply enthusiastic. It wasn't really Woody's fault that he was so hard to control. He was bred to be a hunting dog, and we simply didn't have a year-round facility to provide him with the level of exercise he needed.

Searching for some relief from this canine dynamo, we took him to obedience school.

The class instructor was still gaining experience, and I have a vivid memory of the evening when she said, "Tonight is our off the leash training session."

In the interest of full disclosure I replied with something along the lines of, "This is not a good idea. Woody will not come back when I call him, and he's sure to create chaos for the dozens of other dogs in the other classes."

The instructor reassured me she could handle the situation so I turned him loose to join his classmates. Off he went at warp speed across the armory before executing a flying mount of an unsuspecting show dog that was being groomed at a remote corner of the building. All five classes of dog owners had taken up the chase before we finally managed to get Woody back in harness.

Similar to the off the leash session, the administrators convinced me to let Woody test for his obedience certificate. The test started with a congenial lady cradling a clipboard coming to register Woody. Before I could react Woody showed his welcoming skills by jumping forward to give the volunteer a hug. Her clipboard and all the registration sheets flew in fifty different directions. The outcome was as expected, Woody had produced the lowest score in the history of the 90-year-old armory.

We knew Woody would be a challenge at Comfort Island, and we got a remote control shock collar in advance. Allowing Woody to freewheel without easy intervention was a prescription for chaos. He took his handy electronic gadget swimming a hundred times or so in the first week and the antenna fell off first before it stopped working altogether.

One of the best features of having Woody at Comfort Island was that he could run as much as he wanted without us having to worry about him running off. I did have to discourage him from swimming after ducks a couple of times, but he learned to avoid the swift currents when he wasn't on shore.

He was a powerful dog and he could accelerate up steep slopes that we had trouble scaling at any speed. He loved to ride in the boat, and Coty, Tori and their friends would throw the ball for him endlessly.

He wanted to greet folks by jumping up on them, and it was necessary to restrain him vigilantly when elderly guests came to visit. He would sometimes try to jump on or into a boat that arrived at the dock, which was scary if it was a valuable wooden boat. It was no wonder that during Woody's tenure most callers came in their workboat rather than their Sunday go-to-meeting boat.

CHAPTER 53

❦

The "Home Depot" Restoration Program

REGULAR MAINTENANCE MAKES taking care of a mansion difficult but manageable. We had let our maintenance program slide after Dad died. We did replace the boathouse dock nearest the beach in time for the 1883 centennial celebration with funds we received from selling the *Consuelo*, but we not only had to go to court to gain possession of Comfort Island, we also inherited no funds that would have assisted our maintenance efforts.

New York State has the distinction of levying the highest overall taxes in the country, and the local tax collectors have a predisposition to fleece the islanders who receive no services in return. Deb thought we should sell and move on, and I saw her point.

Indeed, it made my blood boil to be informed that we were considered non-residents and would be required to pay the same rate as a transient tourist for a fishing license. We were paying many thousands of dollars in school taxes to help make the resident teachers the highest paid in the United States, but when we wanted to send Coty through the Driver's Ed Program one summer we got the repetitive, "Sorry, you're not a permanent resident." I wonder how the United States Supreme Court would view the fact that New York State actually adds a surcharge to non-residents' school taxes, but won't allow the individuals to attend the schools they are paying for?

By 1992 Deb had reached a breaking point and she wanted out. The strain of trying to figure out how to coordinate such a complicated project was too much. I told her, "Don't give up, Deb. Kira and I will take over for a while and try to right the ship."

Beginning in 1985 I hired a tennis assistant to help with my group teaching. My first assistant was Tim DiPrinzio. He did a good job, and I was sorry when he moved to Vermont the following year. Peter Henderson was nineteen and one of my former students. He called me about filling the teaching vacancy, and I said I'd take him on for the season and see how it went. It was a excellent decision because he did a fine job assisting my programs that year and for twenty-five years in all before he moved on after 2011.

By 1992, I knew he had become quite handy working on family construction projects because I'd been to their camp and seen some of the work he'd done. It occurred to me that he might be able to help me tackle some the Comfort Island maintenance problems. We assessed what needed to be done and Peter quickly demonstrated that he was an efficient and tireless worker. I paid him what I could his first season at Comfort, and after that he became the third member of the "unpaid help team" along with Kira and me.

Peter Henderson rebuilding dock

It had been thirty years since Dad had initiated the last restoration, and the house was one-hundred-and-ten years old when Peter and I began the "Home Depot" restoration project. The roof needed work, windows on the second floor were deteriorating, the boathouse was being held together with what amounted to a Band-Aid and all the original cement was turning to sand.

One of my tennis students, Jerry Ingerson, was a building contractor and he came to the island after we played doubles one day to assess what needed to be done. He was like our Pomeranian "Brooklyn" chasing chipmunks as he darted around under the house and when he ran around on the roof holding a rope with one hand, I questioned his sanity. I wouldn't have considered walking on that roof no matter how many parachutes and ropes I had attached to me.

It didn't take him long evaluate what needed to be done. I was glad to be sitting down enjoying a frosty, cold beer when he announced, "I could bring my crew out here and put this place back in first rate shape for one-point-four million dollars." I gave that comment a sardonic laugh before Jerry continued on saying, "You have a serious situation on the corner under the dining porch. The timbers are rotten and it looks as though it could collapse at any time. It scares me, and I think something should be done very soon."

If it scared him, it terrified me, and we agreed to barter tennis lessons for having his crew come and rehabilitate the problem area. This was an exception since we hired very little outside help to come work on our projects.

Once the porch corner was repaired, Peter and I addressed the rest of the supports under the house. The stone piers that support the porches were threatening to collapse because the cement was giving way. Peter replaced several of the joists under the front porch first. Next he used jacks to keep the porch in place while he worked his way around the house pointing-up or in some cases starting from ground level rebuilding the rock piers. I remembered Mr. Papworth's explanation about cement returning to powder and sand after eighty years as Peter used a screwdriver and his fingernail to dislodge the antiquated mortar.

I set up a work area on the front lawn where I used a wheelbarrow, a hoe, and a shovel to mix the cement with a garden hose nearby to add water as needed. Peter would reappear from wherever he was working at the moment with a five gallon bucket into which he'd add fresh cement then return to stabilizes the next peer until he had finished circling the house.

We addressed the critical projects first and gradually added a few cosmetic projects for the sake of boosting our morale. The decking on the back porch was another serious problem that couldn't be ignored or even delayed. The wooden surface was rotting, and it got to the point where boards were giving way when someone stepped in the wrong place. It had clearly become dangerous for Kira to carry a wash basket out to the clothesline at the edge of the deck.

John Durand was one of the owners of the Wellesley Island Building Supply, and he agreed to give us a discount on the materials we purchased from his business. We were already becoming volume customers by the time we purchased the lumber to rebuild the back deck, and our formula of buying the materials as cheap as possible and doing the work ourselves was looking like a winner.

Jreck Subs had a long history of being a favorite with our kids. Kira, Peter and I liked them too. I don't know how many days we sat on the front porch having a sub after teaching tennis in the morning and before working on the house during the afternoon, but I'm guessing somewhere between five-hundred and a thousand subs were devoured in that setting. We'd talk about a multitude of topics and a few still stand out in my memory. I remember Peter saying something like, "We don't make a lot of money, but we make enough to be at the river full time. By doing the work ourselves, we don't have to make a big income to pay some fancy building concern to do the work for us. Most men with summer homes in the 1000 Islands have to commute back and forth from some distant job, and they only spend a fraction of the time we do enjoying the river."

Billy Zeigler had headed up an affordable roofing program, but Billy passed away as a young man after losing his battle with cancer, and the business closed. We had kept up with our roofing needs by doing small sections, as needed, but other local roofers were too expensive for our paltry budget. A dormer on the third story hadn't been shingled in many decades and the rafters inside the attic were showing water damage.

We secured a trio of extension ladders rising from a second story bedroom porch with ropes tied to the tower railing and the two chimneys. This set a base for our makeshift scaffolding. Because of the five-sided shape of the dormer roofline, each shingle had to hand-cut and fitted into place.

The plan was for Peter to reroof the dormer then repaint the sides of the structure, and apply new putty to the windows. It became obvious that the season would end before he could finish the three tasks so I reluctantly volunteered to do the cosmetic work. I had been afflicted with grand mal epileptic seizures as a child, which made me very fearful of heights. During this project, I learned not to look down, and I was able to complete the necessary work without incident. To my surprise, after a week or two, I was no longer leaving my fingerprints in the wooden rungs of the ladder or the composition shingles.

Peter was becoming indispensable. He would drain the water in the fall and turn it back on in the spring. He would pull the boats and put on shutters after we left to get Coty and Tori back to Asheville for school.

In 1998 we sold the lower flat to our former neighbor, Hugh Papworth, to generate funds to rebuild the cribs and dock that was on the verge of collapse. The Papworths had sold their share of the island in 1993. I felt badly that some of the clan including Hugh's kids had wanted to stay, and I reasoned that they could still have a presence if we sold to them. We rebuilt the septic to accommodate two dwellings before our season with the kids ended, and then we started the preliminary work for rebuilding the boathouse dock.

Conforming to the school year, which thrived on ever-shorter summer breaks, was an impediment to our restoration effort. For several years during this period we returned to work for a week or two after getting Coty and Tori situated in school.

By the time we returned in mid-September of 1998, Peter had already rebuilt much of the superstructure that supports the dock. He had placed ladders over the rock-filled cribs then took a fireplace log carrier to each timber-enclosed pile of rocks and hiked rocks to shore until he was down to the level where the timbers were no longer rotten. He spliced new 8" x 8" timbers on top of the old ones with foot-long spikes and then hiked the rocks back out across the ladders and refilled the new cribs. A day after we arrived I found myself driving spikes into timbers with a sledgehammer.

Next came driving nails into deck boards on my hands and knees. For someone who had run thousands of miles chasing tennis balls on concrete tennis courts playing former world-class tennis players, my knees in particular said a lot of bad things to me as the project crawled to completion.

In 1999 we addressed replacing and reinforcing the cement work in and around the boathouse. This qualified as some of the hardest physical labor I ever took part in. We returned from Asheville in September, as had become our custom, to undertake this project and to close up.

Peter had a small cement mixer at his family farm that we loaded into his van and brought over to Comfort in the Mad Hatter. I remember straining then laughing as we wrestled with the barrel and I said, "Are you kidding me. This thing is as heavy as a freight train."

Garlock's Hardware delivered thirty-three sacks of cement and a barge load of sand with gravel. We used it all in the process of pouring ten yards of new concrete into the seawall inside the boathouse and the adjoining seawall. The weather did its part to make it a memorable stay with persistent rain and cold temperatures. It was another exhausting non-vacation.

Despite the hard work, Peter had a great sense of humor and I would laugh as he reiterated his motto of, "You can't quit, and you can't be fired."

Our idea was to fix problem areas in such a way that it would be at least forty years before anyone would have to fix it again. This was in contrast to some of the work that Dad had funded with a Band-Aid approach, which had only been intended as a short-term fix to a problem that became a major problem for us later.

CHAPTER 54

⚭

First, Let's Check With the Amish

WE HAD DONE a prodigious amount of structural work by the time the third century of the Clark tenure at Comfort Island began in 2000. We had invested eight years in our restoration program, and most of the work didn't do much to improve the outward appearance aside from the new dock and cement work. Kira was a catalyst in lobbying to initiate a few projects that would make the place look better.

We painted the porch walls, ceilings, decks and the white trim on the window moldings and railings. Peter replaced the dilapidated lattice that enclosed the areas beneath the porches with pressure-treated wood that he sawed into narrow strips and stained at home. The second story windows were on life support and added to the shabby appearance. I asked Peter, "Can you build new windows?"

He said, "I think we should go see if the Amish can make replacement windows for us instead." We removed two of the most decrepit window frames and carefully extracted the wavy, antique glass. Then we covered the vacant window casings with plywood. Tennis season was all but done on the September morning when we began our search for an Amish craftsman that could duplicate the custom sizes and shapes.

We loaded the frames into Peter's prized work vehicle: a brown 1981 Ford Econoline van. The vehicle had been the pride of Henderson family transportation in the early 1980s when Peter and his twin sister, Pam, first came for tennis lessons. Peter along with his mom, dad, grandma, and sister would arrive early to set up aluminum deck chairs so the adults could witness the proceedings in comfort. A decade later, a new van was purchased, and Peter assumed use of the earlier model. Mice spent a winter nesting in the interior lining while Peter resided in Florida, and he removed the lining in the spring. It was literally a bare bones edition, and we'd laugh on a hot day when I'd roll down the window while saying, "Turning on the air conditioning."

I had been wearing a traditional Amish straw hat when I taught tennis since the early 1980s. Peter had bought a hat of his own when he came to work for me in 1986. The hats were handmade, very durable and inexpensive. I paid eight dollars for my first one. The main Amish population in this region was northeast of the 1000 Islands between De Peyster and Heuvelton, New York.

Kira, the kids, and I took drives through the rustic farms the Amish owned on occasion. It was unique seeing one-room schools, men and children plowing their fields with draft horses, people wearing dark purple or black clothing, and the use of a horse and buggy for transportation. The young children would wave excitedly as we drove by. I marveled at how uncluttered the area was around their house and outlying buildings, while the general public in this region was surrounded by personal trash heaps featuring rusted cars, broken farm equipment, and an endless variety of accumulated junk.

Our first stop was the Amish sawmill adjacent to Black Lake. We spoke with the workers there, who suggested that a cabinetmaker a dozen miles up the road near De Peyster might be able to assist us. We found the location without difficulty, but the cabinetmaker explained that he was strictly a cabinetmaker and didn't make windows. He suggested a fellow named Dan Miller who lived above Heuvelton another dozen miles or so from our current location. I recall him saying, "You'll know you are there when you get to a big bend in the road."

I said something to Peter like, "These folks have a very different slant on giving directions. Don't you agree?"

We meandered around several rural roads before we found Mr. Dan Miller's farm. Typical of these farms, we were greeted by dogs and kids. We hauled our derelict windows out of the van and Mr. Miller agreed they were beyond repair. We ordered eight replacement windows. He said, "Send me a letter in the spring to remind me."

The Amish have no electric lights, phones, or other everyday conveniences, and communicating with them is not a simple matter. I did write in the spring, but when Peter and I drove to the farm in June, the windows had not even been started. I reiterated what I wanted and asked Dan what he estimated the cost would be.

He quoted a cost for each linear inch, as he measured around the edges of the frame. Peter and I both laughed when Dan came to a gap in the wood where the wood had rotted out, and he said, "You know I am going to have to charge you for the space that is not here anymore."

I reassured him that was not a problem and he said, "Come back in a week and I'll have the first eight windows ready for you."

Several times we returned with new shapes and sizes for him to duplicate. He made us thirty-three first class window frames, and I paid him a fraction of what it would cost for commercial fabrication.

CHAPTER 55

❧

"It Was the Best of Times"

Family off for ride in Buzz

TORI AND COTY were river rats, and they had a ton of experience in and around boats by the time they reached the minimum age of ten when they took the Safe Boating Course and passed the exam to get their boating licenses. We had a sixteen-foot Polar Craft that was powered by a twenty-five horsepower Evinrude outboard engine. I'd ride along while Coty practiced handling the boat and docking.

Two years later Tori had her license and the practice routine was repeated. By this time Coty was developing an interest in golf in addition to tennis. He took golf lessons from Mike Hebert at the TI Club, and we allowed him to take the "Blue Boat," as we called it, to his lessons, which entailed crossing the main channel. Of course Tori wanted the same privileges even though she was younger. We did allow her to visit her friend Courtney McCullough on Cuba Island a few hundred yards downriver, but she was not allowed to cross the main channel, as had been the rule with Coty when he was her age.

One day Peter and I arrived back at the island after teaching, and to our surprise the outboard engine was lying on the dock with the cover off. I remember saying to Peter, "I can hardly wait to hear this story."

Kira gave Peter and I the gist of the story, while the three of us devoured our daily Jreck Subs. Tori's heartthrob, "Stewie-baby" came to McCullough's to visit Courtney's brother, Alex. Someone suggested a boat ride, and Tori volunteered to do the driving across the main channel toward the TI Club. Before she reached the club she hit a wave awkwardly and the motor jumped off the back of the boat. A lady from Castle Rest Island witnessed the accident, and called Kira to say Tori needed help.

I got the play-by-play from the kids later because I didn't want to drive Kira's blood pressure off the chart by having her revisit the scene a second time. The participants all agreed Kira arrived in a decidedly angry state. She jumped into the shallow water where the motor laid, grabbed the motor and heaved it into the Polar Craft. She climbed out of the water, escorted the three passengers back to Cuba Island and Miss Tori back to Comfort. This was not a light motor and those involved made a mental note not to get on the wrong side of Mrs. Clark.

I have had great fun running tennis programs for kids. There are ebbs and flows to group teaching. Some years there are fewer kids and not much enthusiasm for becoming advanced players, whereas at other times it is the opposite. Back in the late 1970s I had a group of motivated adolescents that shared my excitement about going out and finding kids to play from other programs. After that contingent graduated to more adult roles another group emerged a few years later.

Tennis was reaching another zenith during the late 1990s. Peter had been assisting me at Grenadier since we began the restoration work in 1992, and we had clinics at the club with more than fifteen kids attending on a regular basis. Someone reminded me that we had thirty-five to forty-five kids in Alex Bay during the 1980s. Yes, but we had a much smaller pool to draw from at the club, and these fifteen kids including Tori and Coty were proficient enough to compete for many highly ranked, metropolitan school tennis teams.

I had three programs operating at this time. I had junior groups going at the Grenadier Island Country Club (GICC), Alexandria Bay and Clayton. I invited the advanced players to come play at the Alex Bay courts one afternoon each week. I'd match up players from the three programs to practice and play against each other. Quite often I'd join in and play singles or doubles when I recognized a challenge or wanted to illustrate tactics and strategy.

We had a group in the 1980s that went to Brockville, Ontario to play then we hosted return matches at Alex Bay, but the Brockville club failed financially and that program was defunct. I found an active junior tennis academy program in Kingston, Ontario and we took teams there between 1999 and 2002.

Kingston is a Canadian city about forty miles from Alexandria Bay. Most of our team members were residing in New York, which meant each of us had to cross the border and go through the customs checkpoint. Half a dozen parents drove one or more children across the border that day.

The custom officials sit in a glassed-in booth in front of a computer that scans the license plate and passenger information. Each car waits in line perhaps twenty or thirty feet from the booth then move up to the booth when it is their turn. A scanning device relays the plate information to the agent as the driver moves forward. The official asks, "Where are you coming from? Where are you going? What is the purpose of your trip?" They listen to the driver's response. The agent either tells the driver to proceed with their trip or to pull over to one of the parking spaces in front of the customs building for further questioning and perhaps a search of the vehicle.

The officials want to be able to see into the car, and they ask anyone wearing dark glasses to take them off. The mood is generally serious and any light-hearted conversation is rare indeed. Apparently this day was an exception because we heard reports of the agent asking the usual questions to the first series of cars, but the parents in the last couple of cars reported the official saying, "Yes, I know. You are going to the tennis matches in Kingston" when the agent was able to see tennis rackets and kids dressed in athletic attire.

I remember this initial Kingston outing well. It was one of the hottest days of the summer, and despite a small grandstand next to the courts, spectators and players alike were standing under trees in the shade. We had a large team approaching twenty players while they had ten at the most. Their coach and I paired off some of our most advanced players in featured matches, and then we allowed all the kids to decide who they wanted to play with or against for the next two hours. The kids had a blast and the enthusiasm carried over after the matches ended. Several kids came to me and said, "Coach, some of us want to go for pizza. How about joining us?" A majority of our group met for pizza at one of the quaint waterfront cafes located on King Street.

Kingston marks the eastern terminus of the Great Lakes and Lake Ontario in particular. The view from the outdoor café was spectacular. I recall looking out at the open lake to the southwest and Wolfe Island to the southeast. Wolfe Island is the largest of the 1800 islands with a length of eighteen miles and width that varies from nearly six miles to a few hundred yards. The island is like a sentry at the entrance to the archipelago. A large marina was adjacent to a nearby park providing docking for a dominant sailboat population. The sailing events for the 1976 Montreal Olympics were held in Kingston. It was an interesting city to visit and an excellent venue for our competitive tennis experience.

In early June 2002, a few days after arriving for the season, Kira said, "I'm going to buy a Sea-Doo so we have one of our own to use." Kira's cousin George had a small armada of the Sea-Doo brand jet skis at the family place on Grenadier, and he encouraged us to go riding when we came to visit. We were all experienced riders by the time we bought a jet ski of our own, and it added to the fun the four of us had on the water.

George's grandfather, George Blaisdell, founded the Zippo lighter company. George's two cousins and his brother, Paul, lacked the commitment and motivation to learn the business from the ground up as he had done. Starting in the stockroom as a summer intern during his college days at Louisiana State University then moving up to sales after graduation, George worked his way through the ranks until he eventually owned the entire company. Under his guidance and leadership the company blossomed into a major entity, but he has not been spoiled by his success. He supports many worthy causes without seeking recognition or fanfare, and most of the time he lives by a simple lifestyle.

Many young people like the thrill of going fast, jumping waves and making sharp turns on a jet ski. I liked cruising with friends, like George, while exploring new areas without the worry of doing serious damage to my boat while navigating tricky sections of the river. It gave me a sense of exhilaration as my body hurdled forward through the air with a lifejacket and dark glasses being my only safety equipment. The state I entered into during these rides approached pure euphoria. Motorcyclists speak of similar experiences riding on scenic stretches of back roads.

Coty and Tori shared in the use of our fancy new toy. Coty, in particular, was an exponent of going fast in rough water and leaping over wakes created by cruisers and other deep draft, pleasure craft.

Adolescents can get a permit to work in New York at the age of fourteen and Coty and Tori did so. Getting a summer job was usually the reason a boy or girl in their mid-teens would stop participating in our tennis events. It was a rarity that many of those in Coty and Tori's group continued to come for most or all of their high school years. Coty started working at the 1000 Islands Bait Store in 2002, and he liked the idea of earning his own money.

I remember vividly going with Coty and Kira to American Eagle Outfitters so Coty could buy some new clothes. He was generally very careful to buy things he genuinely needed realizing that we couldn't afford to squander money on unnecessary purchases. However on this occasion he heaped an impressive assortment of pants and shirts onto the counter. Kira questioned whether he really needed all the new clothes at which time he took the funds out of his wallet and said, "I earned this money, and this is what I want to spend it on."

It made me appreciate what a fine young man he had become, and I was proud to say that we had raised him.

CHAPTER 56

--- ❧ ---

"Brooklyn," Our First Good Dog

Brooklyn

LAST ON MY chronological list of extra special Comfort Island dogs was our Pomeranian named Brooklyn (2004-2012). He was a predominantly black tricolor with white markings mostly around his neckline and two little brown eyebrows. He weighted about fourteen pounds. I'd chuckle as I announced, "He's the first good dog we've ever had."

Brooklyn was at Comfort during the later days of Woody's tenure along with another Black Lab we had at the time named "Pudge." Woody weighed ninety-three pounds and Pudge was bigger than Woody. When Pudge and Brooklyn were both young pups, they would tear around the lawns playing catch-me-if-you-can. Brooklyn was as quick as lightning scampering one way then dodging another. Around they'd go, and maybe once or twice a day Pudge would manage to catch his smaller tormentor by the tail, whereupon he'd sling the little fella like a Frisbee.

When we'd leave our trio of dogs alone, they developed the unwelcome hobby of turning over the trashcan and scavenging for choice leftovers. Brooklyn would greet us as we returned from shore. He'd strut up the hill to the kitchen where we'd discover Pudge and Woody wallowing on a floor covered with garbage. The two culprits would hang their guilty heads while we scolded them.

Pudge standing watch at beach

One day I said, "Let's pretend to leave then slip around to the back porch to see just how these four-legged miscreants work their operation."

We peeked through the back screened-door. Woody and Pudge were nowhere in sight, only Brooklyn was casing out the trash receptacle. Suddenly he sprung several feet up into the air and hooked his front paws over the top of the plastic container thus toppling it to the floor. He sifted through the debris picking out choice morsels. When he'd had his fill, he demonstrated his real genius by going to fetch his two buddies to clean up the dregs. Pudge and Woody had been taking the rap for Brooklyn's handiwork from the start.

Brooklyn became something of a legend at GICC as we began spending more time at the house on Grenadier. Members would stop from time-to-time in their golf cart to report, "He came and jumped in the cart and rode a few holes with us. He acted as though we were lifelong friends." I have taught tennis there for nearly forty years and Brooklyn often joined me at the courts to wait for his next unconventional activity.

He got to know the workers on a first name basis, and Gordie was his favorite. I often stood and watched as Brooklyn spied the cart carrying the mowers headed to the maintenance shed. As the trailer backed toward the ramp, Brooklyn knew it was his signal to gallop across the number three green and up the grassy knoll to the shed entrance. If the weather was cold and the door was shut, he would scratch to be let in.

Gordie was a true dog lover, and he'd bring a pork chop, meat patties or some other special treat for Brooklyn. Once his treat-break was completed, Brooklyn would trot back to the courts, and resume his sentry duty to see what fun he might enjoy next.

Dogs are a reminder of our own mortality since their lifespan is relatively short compared to humans. Brooklyn suffered from a heart murmur that became an enlarged heart. He died prematurely at the age of eight, but I must say he got the most out of life. He had "character."

CHAPTER 57

─────── ⌀ ───────

"It Was the Worst of Times"

THE OPENING OF *A Tale of Two Cities* by Charles Dickens has much to say about a person's mortal journey; "It was the best of times, it was the worst of times."

Our kids were growing up, and life was about to change radically for the Clarks and our future at Comfort Island.

The fabric of our carefree existence was starting to show wear when in October of 2002, Kira was diagnosed with breast cancer. Doctors performed surgery and six months of treatment followed. It turned out that an unscrupulous insurance agent misrepresented the product he had sold us. We filed two formal complaints with the North Carolina Insurance Commissioner, but the complaints were rejected, and it was obvious that we were simply unwitting victims in another example of political corruption.

We were forced to spend critical funds we had saved. We got some relief from medical assistance programs that pitch in for people in situations like ours, but it could have been much worse if Kira's generous cousin George hadn't come to our financial rescue. The bad news was we thought we had catastrophic medical insurance that would protect us against present and future calamities, and this would obviously not be the case going forward.

It was the middle of June before Coty, his friend Josiah Hyatt, and I arrived at the river. Kira came a few days later with her younger sister, Laura, and Laura's daughter, Alexandra. Tori talked us into letting her stay with her friend, Brittany Baldwin, and Brittany's family until later in the summer. Coty returned to the Bait Store part time and Tori and Brittany came for the final three weeks of the season.

We were on our way to Sarasota to spend the Christmas holiday with Kira's mom when we got a call from Kira's older sister, Debra, saying Grandma had passed away in her sleep during the night.

Coty was accepted at the University of Tampa with an academic scholarship and was in the process of taking his final exams when he reported he'd been having pain in his left knee. We sent him to see our family doctor who sent him for more tests. The doctor told us there was reason for concern, and we immediately became involved with the ongoing doctors visits.

It was determined that Coty had been stricken with osteosarcoma or bone cancer. He went through a regimen of chemotherapy that lasted seven months. Our 2004 season at Comfort Island consisted of a brief visit one afternoon by Kira and me. Cousin George flew all of us plus Coty's friend, Josiah Hyatt, up on a private charter jet for five days between treatments. We stayed at his new residence on Grenadier Island before returning to Asheville so Coty could undergo the next round of chemotherapy. The treatments would continue through January 2005.

Dr. Ward, who was the Wake Forest Surgical specialist in charge of the case, deemed amputation of the affected limb the only possible solution. The surgery was carried out in September 2004. It was a crushing blow for someone showing so much promise for a productive future in theatre.

The Clark family turmoil had broken the floodgates, and the next episode involved Tori who delivered a baby girl, Hailee Skye Lane, on April 21, 2005 at the age of seventeen. Many parents cherish the thought of becoming grandparents, and we were happy to welcome Hailee as a sixth generation of Clark descendants at Comfort Island. We also recognized it would be difficult for Tori to lead a more conventional life as a young adult.

Coty went into remission following his treatments and the amputation, so we returned to Comfort Island in 2005.

We had a party at Comfort for my sixtieth birthday on September 3, 2006, and we took Coty to Turning Stone Resort Casino to celebrate his twenty-first birthday eight days later. He had not been feeling well at the end of the summer, and he went to see the doctor after returning to Asheville.

A feeling of foreboding was overwhelming for both Kira and me. I remember saying, "I think we need to close the island pronto and head for Asheville as quickly as possible."

We closed the island and were back in Asheville within four days. Tests the day after we returned confirmed that the cancer had returned spreading to his lungs, which was a frequent progression of the disease. Prospects for his survival were not good. We scoured the Internet while conferring with Coty's oncologists Dr. Beaty and Dr. Bottom. An experimental program designed by Dr. David Loeb at Johns Hopkins Hospital in Baltimore offered a shred of hope and we went there.

Typical of the way things were going, Coty's insurance ran out when he turned twenty-one. A friend from a neighboring island, who was also one of my former tennis students, called when he heard of Coty's relapse. I told him, "The hospital is withholding treatment until they have assurance that they will be paid."

Donald and Elaine Textor made arrangements to pick up the entire bill.

Four months later on February 12, 2007 Coty passed away.

CHAPTER 58

---- ⌗ ----

Moving On

IT WAS SURELY the emptiest feeling I'd ever experienced when Coty's courageous battle ended. As a parent, I invested the best of what I had to give emotionally, and I did whatever I could to bring out the superior qualities he possessed. The way he dealt with his unfortunate circumstances was a testament to his character, and he won the admiration of many, even those who only had casual contact with him.

We had been staying at a Baltimore Inner Harbor condominium complex near Federal Hill. Visually it was a nice setting with docks in front of the condominiums and a view of ships and other boats entering the waterfront. A Domino Sugar factory was across the harbor, and we'd watch ships tie up and unload for a period of several days before moving out to make room for the next ship. There was a small balcony where I'd sit and watch the activity in the busy waterway. At night the letters of a giant sign erected on top of the factory were lighted in yellow with "Domino" in italics and "Sugar" below it etched in standard print. The border of the sign was illuminated in a reddish-orange.

There was a restaurant named Lilies and a coffee shop named the Barista in the complex. Coty was confined to a wheelchair and needed oxygen and a mask to breathe. When he felt up to it, he'd get someone to wheel him down to the Barista for a Red Bull and something sweet to eat. I remember one morning when the proprietor asked Coty how he was doing. Coty lifted his mask to speak and replied, "I'm doing great! How are you doing?"

The cheerful manner in the way Coty spoke made quite an impression on the owner who was preoccupied with his own personal problems when Coty made his comment.

We all did everything within our power to work a miracle. Coty battled without complaint, and the most negative remark I recall him making was, "I guess you could say, I won the reverse-lottery."

I recall more than one instance when I said to Coty, "None of us lives forever. In the big scheme of time our life on earth is but a blip whether we live to be ten or one hundred." As someone who has lived two-thirds of a century, I can attest that it seems like yesterday that I was ten.

It is hard to know how to return to the real world after enduring such a period of darkness. Teaching tennis had not made me rich financially, but I had accrued benefits that few ever attain otherwise. Giving thanks for those that are there for us during trying times is always time well spent. Cousin George, Donald and Elaine Textor, and a host of other personal friends did what they could to ease our burden, and we were truly grateful. Another of my tennis students and one of my favorite people was Edith Amsterdam. She was over eighty when Coty passed on, and I was well aware that she had lost two of her four children in recent years. I called her to ask her indulgence in sharing with me how she dealt with her own personal tragedies.

She counseled me by saying, "You can go sit in a dark room and feel sorry for yourself, or you can move on with your life. Bring Kira, and come spend a few days with me at my Curry Mansion Inn Bed & Breakfast in Key West."

We held a memorial service at Comfort in July with many of our River friends attending. Our neighbor from across the shipping channel, Marty Yenowine, conducted the service and Tori's former singing teacher, Kathryn Ingerson, sang several arias. Deb spoke briefly and so did I.

Deb spoke about the irony of our great grandparents coming five generations before this occasion after losing their only daughter, and now we were gathered to celebrate the life of another Clark who had died way too young.

I repeated a story I'd been told about Coty and his fondness for Jreck Subs. Coty and a number of his friends would go to town for a Jreck Sub every day they possibly could. One summer Coty made it forty-five days in a row. During the course of that streak, he forgot his wallet one day. He was embarrassed when he found he had no funds to pay for the sandwich, but the proprietor only laughed and said, "No problem, Coty. I'll paste the slip here, and you can pay for it when you come in tomorrow."

During the fall of 2007 Tori married Sam Naimark, and on May 28, 2008 we welcomed a second granddaughter: Elizabeth "Ellie" Naimark, into the family.

While we thought Coty might find a way to fund and care for Comfort Island if we could hold on long enough, we did not have the same confidence in Sam. Sam had little interest in education or a steady job.

Deb and Ellen-Betsy wanted to sell. In the fall of 2008 I reluctantly agreed, and we put Comfort Island up for sale.

CHAPTER 59

⁂

Want a Great Location and a Project Too?

WE HAD A generous offer from our neighbor, Jim Cumming, in 2007, but we turned it down because we were at a loss about what to do so soon after Coty's passing. The deal was also structured in a way that made us a little uneasy. It was probably a mistake not to take that offer, and it was surely a mistake to ask for significantly more than the first offer when we did the actual listing.

The economy was not doing well when we listed Comfort, and to make matters worse taxes were rising at a rate that made government spending and inflation look tame by comparison. Between 2006 and 2007 the ambitious local assessor more than tripled the taxable value of our property along with many other islanders. We had to hire an attorney and take our case to the New York State Supreme Court to get relief. Our finances had taken a serious hit with our medical and insurance nightmares, and the horrendous school and property taxes combined made it impossible to do much-needed work.

A property like ours needed a prosperous buyer who had an interest in restoring those subtle elements that constitute grandeur in a completed project. A brand new house with all the modern conveniences is what many people identify as being the ultimate, but it takes imagination to see the beauty in something less than shiny new.

Seeing the Comfort Island house preserved constituted my primary goal. The realtor we picked, Mike Franklin, had a background in historical real estate and a talent for photography. He used the Internet to create exposure for the property with some interesting results.

The house was featured in a number of national venues including *The Wall Street Journal*, a Merv Griffin television production called "It Costs What?" and *Private Islands* magazine.

The Alexandria Township Historical Society wanted to mount an impressionist exhibition of Alson S. Clark's artwork. We made numerous materials available for that exhibit, which was on display in 2009 and 2010. This added exposure to the property and the house where his murals graced various walls on both the first and second floors.

It had been five years since we had done serious work on the house and with a place that big and that old, maintenance work needs to be done on a yearly basis if the intent is to keep it in first class shape.

The quick sale we had envisioned was not forthcoming. The ceilings were starting to leak and plaster was cracking and falling in some places. The place needed sprucing up to attract a willing buyer. As the 2011 season ended with no offers on the property, Kira and I discussed the situation, "Well Tad, another year has passed and not a single bid. What do you propose to do? The house is looking shabby and we can't go on forever waiting for your ideal buyer."

"I know, but I'm not willing to give the place away without doing everything I can to find a person who will appreciate the setting and the history."

Peter was an infrequent visitor now, and he signed off as my assistant teaching pro after the 2011 season. Peter assisted on the courts and at the house from 1986 – 2011, and he surely had the second longest tenure of anyone who worked for the Clarks at Comfort Island. George Root's seventy-year stint as caretaker is a record that is hard to imagine anyone approaching much less surpassing, but Peter certainly had a major role in extending the length of our presence on Comfort Island.

I no longer felt the same enthusiasm working for the benefit of a venue that would sooner or later belong to someone else. I was old enough to collect social security by the time we listed, and tackling the workload that had kept several hired men busy in the days of my great grandparents became an insurmountable task. Had I retired from teaching tennis I could have accomplished more, but teaching tennis was my passion and I wasn't about to give that up. The lilacs and sumac were taking back some of the ground I'd won from them a decade or two before. Even the yard was starting to look rundown.

The Comfort abode was designed with warm summer days and paid help in mind. We had a furnace, but we stopped using it in 1983. We only had a manual dishwasher and ninety-nine percent of the time the brand name was "Kira." We were spending more time at Grenadier each year after the house there was remodeled in 2008. In the spring and the fall it was luxurious having the ability to simply turn a dial for heat, push a button to accomplish the dishwashing chore, and to have a caretaker to do the heavy lifting.

Cousin George assisted the Comfort Island cause when our finances began showing unsustainable strain, but we could all see that our continuing ownership simply didn't make sense. I hadn't the interest, training or youthfulness to embark on a new career that would pay me what was needed to effect a full restoration then sustain the growing maintenance expenses.

CHAPTER 60

❀

Can an Island Have Nine Lives?

AFTER THIS LENGTHY period of gloom that included losing Coty then making the decision to sell the island, a revival of sorts took place as though Comfort was the cat with nine lives and wanted to treat one more generation of Clarks to the magic of its unique setting.

Author and wife on front porch

Each new generation of kids has taken varying levels of interest in the obvious activities of fishing, swimming, and boating, but it's interesting to reflect back on the earliest generation who set a precedent for creative entertainment. Readymade toys like model boats, kites, radios and computing devices weren't available in 1883.

My great uncle, Alson, built box kites that eventually developed into elaborate designs that supported a camera, and he produced aerial photographs long before the Wright brothers embarked on their first flight at Kitty Hawk in 1903. During World War I he did aerial reconnaissance for the United States Army over German-held territory in France. Glass plates of his photography still exist at Comfort Island.

My grandfather, Mancel, fashioned wooden boat models by hand with crude tools, which served as a precursor to his passion for boating and cruising in particular. I still have a scale model of his cruiser *Sabot* that he created from wood around 1920.

The youngest brother, Eddie, was a child prodigy on the banjo and piano, and he was the catalyst for the three boys hosting "evening attic entertainment" in the late 1880s. Eddie later was elected president of the Yale Banjo Club, and after graduation he gained notoriety for being able to attend a musical production one time and then repeat the entire score from memory on the piano.

Tori was preoccupied with her family, nonetheless she was not pleased by the prospect of losing her brother and her Comfort Island heritage too. The island had been an anchor of continuity in her life and the memories were dear to her. In an ignorant way, I underestimated how important it was to be more involved with Tori. In retrospect it seemed that we paired off by gender. I spent more time mentoring Coty, though Kira spent time mentoring both kids, she spent far more time with Tori than I did. Now that I have grown to know Tori better, I realize that she is every bit as special and irreplaceable as her brother.

She was a certified river rat, and her two daughters were destined to become river rats too. Outdoor activities and generating their personalized form of amusement were a part of our river culture and family heritage. We have never had any television service at Comfort Island and that was by design. It is a sad development that the emphasis for kids has switched to someone else force-feeding entertainment rather than kids taking an active role in entertaining themselves.

Tori, Hailee and Ellie began coming for three week stretches during mid-summer beginning in 2009. Tori was already experiencing marital problems with Sam. They separated in December of 2009, and their divorce became final in 2011. Tori moved back home, and the girls spent their apportioned time with their "mommy" and us too.

It is pleasing to be able to enjoy grandchildren when one is still energetic enough to interact with them. While it was difficult for Tori to have children so young, Kira and I viewed having grandchildren in a positive light. We had lost our precious son, but we gained two wonderful granddaughters. I'm pretty sure there is no way to turn this into a mathematical formula because I do know there is no substitute for losing a child. Our life went on and we continued to be thankful for each new blessing.

As I have watched Hailee and Ellie make up games and spin their version of shared fantasy, I see a decided difference in the themes they embrace compared to Coty and Tori at corresponding ages. Coty and Tori played "restaurant" with their stuffed animals. Hailee and Ellie used the same black wooden hope chest with a new cast of characters to play domestic games with their "babies."

The new games were about feeding and interacting with their newborn infants. Hailee held her baby doll up to her shoulder patting it on the back while saying, "I think she is spitting up."

Ellie looked down at the infant she had cradled in a blanket and offered her motherly evaluation, "My baby doesn't like his cereal."

I have often wondered if the cast of characters is influenced by the gender of the children involved? If a boy and a girl played with stuffed animals and two girls played with babies, what would two boys play with or would they be attracted to a table scene at all?

Being married to Kira is another blessing. She has had a special gift when it comes to interacting with kids. I loved to watch her read, color, play make-believe and simply orchestrate common daily events for Tori and Coty and now Hailee and Ellie. In a similar way that I am able to connect with kids on the tennis courts, Kira connects by thinking up fun ways to approach everyday activities.

"I'm going down to the beach. Anyone want to join me?" Kira would say.

"We want to go!" Hailee and Ellie typically squealed with delight.

Kira would help them on with their swimsuits and off they'd go with a detour to the boathouse to collect beach toys and floatable devices. Some of the toys had survived from Coty and Tori's generation, and they were just as relevant for the new generation as they had been for the one before. The girls would play in the sand with buckets, shovels and other assorted toys at the water's edge along with Brooklyn who was delighted to join in on the festivities.

Beach weather generally indicated swimming weather, and "Granna," Tori, Hailee, Ellie, and Brooklyn bounded into the water like it was a tub full of bathwater. Air mattresses, life rings and floating plastic animals added to the fun. It was a rarity when "Grandpa" ventured into the water at all. I regarded seventy-five degree water as ice cold, and it took me at least ten minutes to get all the way in to start swimming. It has always amazed me that kids show no signs of having a sensor that tells them the water is too darn cold to go swimming.

CHAPTER 61

꙳

Moonrise Kingdom

COMFORT ISLAND BECAME quite a lively spot in conjunction with the publicity it received after we listed it for sale. One fall day in 2010 a young woman pulled up to our dock in a rental boat. She said, "Excuse me, sir. I'm part of a production team that's preparing to make a movie next year and our set director, Adam Stockhausen, is interested in your house. He saw photos of the house interior on the Internet. Is it okay if I come ashore and take a few shots of the Victorian cottage?"

I had no idea who Adam Stockhausen was but the idea intrigued me and I said, "Come ahead."

After her visit I did a little Internet research regarding the upcoming movie that was to be titled *Moonrise Kingdom*. Bruce Willis, Edward Norton and Bill Murray were to join director, Wes Anderson, in the production. Mr. Anderson had previously directed several films including The Royal Tenenbaums, which was nominated in 2001 for the Academy Award for Best Original Screenplay.

Mr. Stockhausen contacted me in mid-November 2010 to ask my permission to come have a personal look at the interior. I advised him that we had returned to North Carolina for the winter some weeks before. Since we had a roofing team still working on the island, and I knew that the front door shutter had not yet been secured for the winter, I gave him permission to tour the house. He did indeed tour the house and took at least 100 photos of furniture and other items that were of interest to him.

He called me after this visit and then again in January to say planning for the movie was going according to schedule and that he was interested in using some of our contents. During the last week in March, I received a file identifying the more valuable contents the production company wanted to borrow. I spoke to Kris Moran who was an associate of the movie company producing the movie and she said they wanted to send a team to remove the contents on April 1st. I thought to myself, "April Fools' Day…how fitting."

I was still in North Carolina, and I'd heard that ice was still in the bays at the river. The moving project sounded monumental to me, and we had some valuable items including the Alson Clark impressionist artwork that I wasn't prepared to loan out without some assurance I'd get everything back. Within a matter of hours another associate provided me with an umbrella policy insuring the contents that were to be removed. The correspondence was now arriving faster than email spam when the legal department emailed me a Permission Release Form. Within a couple of hours all the official matters were completed and the project moved forward.

For those of us that contend with inefficiency from businesses and government on a regular basis, this was an impressive performance just from an organizational standpoint. They formed a team headed by Bob Schleinig to come pack up the desired contents on April 1st. Steve Keeler, a local marina operator, had been commissioned to provide the first day transportation. On April 2nd the team was transported by rented barge back to Comfort Island. The chosen contents were loaded then barged to a waiting moving van in Alexandria Bay. I marveled that all of this was accomplished before the boating season had even begun in the 1000 Islands. I asked Bob, how the production company managed such efficiency. He said, "All it takes is lots of money."

It was a bit of a shock six weeks later when we arrived for the season and realized the extent of the items that were visiting Rhode Island. Our spice rack was gone, our ironing board and butcher block too. Our colander was gone in addition to guest beds and all of our dining room chairs. Numerous pieces of porch furniture were gone, tables throughout the house were gone and kitchen chairs were gone too. It challenged our creativity to exist with so many key items missing and any thought of entertaining guests was out of the question.

I gave Mr. Stockhausen a call and asked him, "How long will we be camping out in our 6500 square foot cottage with almost no furniture?"

He laughed then said, "We expect to finish shooting around the end of June and we'll return your contents promptly when we're done."

Getting our contents returned resulted in a second logistical puzzle. There was the mutually convenient "when" to select. I was at the boathouse preparing to head to work at 8 a.m. on July 12th when a barge approached. I thought it was the phone company coming to repair our line, but I soon realized it was the first barge load of our contents coming home.

I explained that I had to go to work but I'd return around noon. I noted from Bob Schleinig's card that he was a set director as well as a leadman. I told him the house was for sale and to feel free to stage whatever items he deemed appropriate and to leave the extraneous contents in the boathouse.

When the work was concluded the next afternoon, I had the crew sign our guest book in keeping with the tradition that began in 1883. I asked Bob where the movie was filmed and he said, "The set was in Middletown, Rhode Island. It's just off Aquidneck Island and a few miles from Newport. The dwelling is called Clingstone Mansion and it covers a large rock or small island on Narragansett Bay."

I asked him, "What was the purpose of using our contents in the film?"

He said, "The set designers created sets based on the Comfort Island interior and we placed the contents to support these sets."

I asked Bob if he had anything more to add and he responded by saying, "I developed a special feeling for the overall setting and for your long family history at this seemingly unchanged venue. It was a unique experience seeing the place and being a part of it for a few days. I was able to bring that sense of atmosphere to the set when the actual shooting took place."

CHAPTER 62

―――― ✂ ――――

The Zooks Have Landed

By 2010 THE roof at Comfort Island was beginning to look like a ski slope complete with moguls and small jumps. Sky lights weren't necessary as it was easy to see ample daylight through any of the rooms with open rafters or in bedrooms where plaster had fallen from the ceilings. The season was winding down and the house interior would not weather another harsh winter in upper New York State.

A funny aside occurred during the process of finding someone to do the job. At the beginning of October, I stopped my car on the shoulder of Route 12 near Alexandria Bay in order to question two Amish brothers riding along in their buggy about their willingness to tackle a roof project.

A lull of a week or so followed as I waited for various other prospective roofers to give me quotes. One day on the way to town from Grenadier I stopped by Comfort to pick up some business correspondence, and from the walkway I noticed something shut between the screened front doors. It turned out to be a strip of newspaper with a note written on the blank portion between pages. Jonas and Daniel Zook left me the note that said, "Come to look at roof job."

I knew that they would not ride in any motorized boat, and I was curious to know how in the world they got out to the island. I went to their house to discuss having them do part of the job, and I asked them if perhaps they had swum across. They laughed and said "We borrowed a rowboat and loaded it into our buggy. We launched it at the park across from your island and rowed across to have a look."

Had it been earlier in the season the Zooks clearly would have been the low cost provider of choice but rowing them across early each morning in October, November and maybe even December would have been beyond unpleasant. And when the weather was too uncivilized to work, they have no phones, so I'd have been forced to drive eight miles to their farm to say, "See you tomorrow."

We had waited too late in the season for the Zooks to do the job so we had a commercial roofer seal the roof instead. As 2011 began, we were still desperate for help with basic tidy-up projects. I tracked down Jonas and Daniel Zook at the end of June and convinced them that a second trip to Comfort Island would be even better than the first. I assured them that world-renowned skiff racer, Kira Clark, would ferry them to Comfort Island in style.

I paved the way with a visit to the tollbooth at the state park entrance. I questioned whether it would be okay for our workers to be admitted without charge and suggested that their sweet brown mare, "Martha," would likely help with grass-cutting chores while her masters were at Comfort Island.

The park gate-tender wasn't too sure about the whole idea, but she eventually said, "We'll let them in without the fee."

Tools, toolboxes and five-gallon buckets of lunch all were carefully placed on the floorboards of the *Bobby* for the trip. Kira was equal to the task, and in less than ten minutes she had rowed them to the island.

We had expended considerable time and energy getting the Zooks on site to work, and I saw no reason to sugarcoat the first project we needed done. Bat manure had once again grown to grotesque proportions during the intervening twenty-five years since it was cleaned out the previous time. I had purchased the full line of breathing safety equipment in advance, and they selected their preference. They got started on the task with the shovel they brought and a snow shovel I procured on my own.

Two-plus hours and fifteen giant garbage bags later the floor was returned to a respectable state. There was probably half a ton of "AAA" bat fertilizer in those bags, and it could have gone to a grow some great corn except that the roofers had scattered too many nails and partial shingles on the floor to make the blend acceptable to any discerning farmer.

After six hours I paid them for seven to account for "Travel time one way," and I realized the levy was a fraction of what I might have paid otherwise.

"See you next Thursday," I said as the skiff sped downriver toward the well-rested horse that awaited them for the buggy ride home.

CHAPTER 63

The Search For a New Steward Continues

Comfort Island sunrise

WE HAD TEMPORARILY stopped the roof from leaking in 2010, and we had taken steps to make the premises look more presentable early in 2011. The property wasn't selling, and our patience was being tested. Our agent's real estate firm encouraged us to put the property up for auction to coincide with the Clayton Antique Boat Show in August 2011. The auction would be under the direction of another company associate, and we agreed to deposit funds to be used for advertising. If the property sold, our advertising expense would be returned. Our realtor would still receive his above-marketplace commission, and their associate would receive a premium added onto the selling price. We agreed on a reserve minimum and they solicited an opening bid, but no bid was forthcoming by the appointed date, and the auction was abandoned.

At the end of September our realtor and his firm hosted a media event featuring home furnishings designer, Richard McKenzie-Childs. Grandiose plans to have their guest arrive by plane with news reporters on the scene to provide coverage and fanfare went awry when it rained.

Mr. McKenzie-Childs arrived by car instead. The realty company had a photographer at Comfort to record the event and a hostess too. I conducted a thorough tour for our noted guest. He found favor with the carved black trunk that had served as the table for the game of "restaurant" three decades before, but he showed little enthusiasm for the artwork or unusual items like the canvas mailbag. Whimsy, bright pastel colors and outlandish designs were the specialty of our guest and the Comfort interior was not a template for those trendy new styles.

In unsolicited comments tendered to our realtor the day after his visit, Mr. McKenzie-Childs noted the "commanding view" but had little else positive to say about the property. The press coverage was flawed by inaccuracies in one of the featured articles.

In assessing the situation at the end of the 2011 season, I noted that the property had now been listed for three years and interest had actually waned from my perspective. Showings were rare and a request for a viewing was often within an hour or two of when I received the call. One afternoon curiosity seekers arrived with our realtor without an appointment. Kira was at the house alone, and neither of us was pleased that our agent would bring totally unqualified buyers to the property without our approval.

Our rapport with our agent was in decline. We were providing the transportation in some cases after our realtor's boat developed mechanical problems that were never resolved. We hadn't received a single serious offer, and my sisters, Kira and I were all becoming disenchanted with the realty firm. I had been forced into a corner of my own design because I had argued for a realtor that would promote the historic preservation of the house. At yearend I said, "I want to give our realtor one more year, and if the property doesn't sell in 2012, I'll agree to a change."

The Zooks returned to do more cosmetic work in 2012. We decided that repainting the white trim in the kitchen and on the porches would produce the best results for what we had available to spend.

I marveled at how diligent these fellows were. They took no coffee breaks and their lunch hour was over in twenty minutes. They gave the attic floor a second cleaning then moved on to the onerous task of scraping paint. For three days of at least six hours each day, they scraped paint from railings, moldings and trim. After new white stain was applied the exterior looked fantastic.

It had been two years since we had re-sheeted the roof and added the Grace water guard. Leaks were developing again, and it was past time to re-shingle the roof. The roofing contractor, Kyle Felder, also recommended replacing the cedar shakes around the third story dormers while the crew was set-up on the roof.

Kira and I assumed a new role in our capacity as the two remaining stalwarts of the unpaid help team. We were put in charge of painting the shakes and devising ways to dry them quickly so the carpentry crew could work uninterrupted refurbishing the dormers. We each had a plastic three-gallon bucket that we poured paint into. Next we dipped a shingle into the solution before spreading the paint uniformly with a brush.

We tried various methods for drying the painted shakes, which was made more difficult by the cold, rainy weather. We turned several shutters on their sides and leaned wet shakes against them. We also hung shakes from the two clotheslines. We had volunteered to paint four bundles of the cedar shakes, but the crew kept calling for more. It wasn't long before we had done eleven bundles and they were calling for more yet.

We had begun painting shakes before the actual roofing crew arrived, and after more than two weeks of preparing the shakes in windy, cold, and rainy conditions, they fired us for not keeping up. This was the height of irony. How can you fire someone who isn't getting paid?

Our association with the carpenters was doomed from the start. Kira and I treated each red-cedar shake like it was a member of our family, and then a worker would haul an eight-gallon plastic bucket of our premium finished product to the third floor roof where a carpenter would cut three inches off the side of an 18" x 8" shake before pitching the unused portion forty feet to the ground below.

We reasoned that being fired relative to this project was fine by us, and to show I had no hard feelings I filled the eight-gallon bucket one last time with painted shakes I collected off the ground that only had a small section missing on one side or the other.

The carpenters opted to nail the final rows of second-story shakes on without paint, and then paint them after. But when it came to finishing the third-story dormers, it was our turn to laugh, "Look Kira the carpenter's helper is scavenging more of our discarded shakes from the lawn."

Kira added, "I bet they would hate to think we noticed."

CHAPTER 64

❦

How Do You Clear Out a Mansion?

WHEN WE PUT the property on the market in 2008, Kira and I began the monumental task of clearing out generations of the Clarks' personal belongings from the house. The accumulation of "stuff" in the Comfort Island mansion fit the definition of overwhelming. For one hundred and thirty years clothes, artifacts, and wares of every description had been brought to the island and almost nothing had left. A solution to streamlining what one wanted to keep became more difficult after the local community banned burning. In some of the seldom-used closets we found bags of trash that never made it as far as the first floor.

Books, papers, photographs, letters, furniture, linens, clothes and much more were still found in abundance. A hopelessly broken chair didn't go to the dump. Instead it found a new home under the house. Victorian trunks that resemble sofas extending to the floor but having no backs are bursting with puffed sleeved blouses, petticoats and ankle-length skirts. I marveled at an exquisite white lace parasol that Kira retrieved from the closet at the corner of the living room. At least a half-dozen century old peaked captain's hats are found in closets and trunks throughout the house, which gives testament to their popularity for the men of that period.

I found boxes full of papers, letters, photos, and other memorabilia that still had shipping stamps affixed verifying that they had been sent to the island by a relative who wanted to clean out a closet, attic, or storage unit. Dad passed away in 1981, and I remember Ellen-Betsy telling me about sending at least one box herself. She said, "I went to Dad's storage facility after he passed away and a title wave of junk cascaded toward me when I opened the door. Among other things, I found a grocery bag full of junk mail and solicitations from the 1966." I was thankful she threw that out rather than sending it along too.

I took a cursory look in this assemblage of mementoes in the "antique room," and then quickly moved on to simpler project locations like those drawers full of old clothes that I'd tucked away forty years before with the idea I would soon fit into that swell pair of corduroy pants again that looked so good on me when I was eighteen.

When it comes to finding a convenient place to depot that pair of corduroy pants, it is handy to live in a mansion. The room I used as my office didn't even look crowded despite a trunk, three tables, several chairs, and three separate chests of drawers. I opened the closet in the corner of that room, and I was stunned as I took stock of the contents littering the floor. Three tiers of antiquated shoes were heaped on top of each other. Two pairs of hiking boots I'd hardly ever worn were conspicuous on the bottom level. Dress shoes from high school and the years that followed constituted another layer. Near the top of the knee-high pile was a pair of boat shoes.

As I contemplated the task of moving these shoes off the island, I became interested in the history of my footwear as it related to Comfort Island. One of my preferred winter activities was hiking. From the mid-1960s through most of the 1970s I would bring my latest pair of hiking boots to the island thinking I'd drive to the Adirondacks or another hiking location for some serious backpacking. It took me a number of years to realize that the reason I liked to hike in my winter locations was to get to a scenic spot to enjoy the beauty and serenity. A few outings to the mountains in New Hampshire and the Adirondacks made it clear that black flies and mosquitos thrive in those settings. I reflected on how it was a bonus that Comfort Island had no black flies and the mosquito population was almost non-existent thanks to the army of bats that inhabited the attic. As I pondered my motivation for hiking in this region,

I realized that the pretty settings I yearned for could be had as nearby as the front porch.

Next I sorted through my leather-soled dress shoes. I remembered taking a couple of nasty falls with slick, leather-soled shoes. Deb broke her ankle one summer while wearing a pair of leather-soled shoes. Her foot slid out as she walked toward the boathouse on a steep section of the flagstone path.

Off the top of the pile, I fished out the one pair of boat shoes that had never been able to break in properly. I became curious about why this particular style of shoe became my preferred footwear when at the river. I decided to see just how many pairs I had. I discovered a second pair in the closet, two more pairs were at the edge of a bureau, I knew I had a pair downstairs, and I almost forgot the pair I was wearing. I counted six pairs in all.

I cajole my bride about her Amelda Marcos appetite for shoes, yet here I was with six pairs all of one style. At least her ninety-nine pairs are different styles, brands and colors. The same could not be said of my collection of footwear called "boat shoes." Boat shoes have a skid resistant, rubber sole, and the upper looks like a blend between a loafer and a moccasin with a rawhide thong that is threaded through eyelets and ties at the tongue. The fit can be made more or less snug by tightening or loosening the leather lace.

I really can't remember when I bought my first pair of boat shoes, but I do know I made the purchase at Folino's Shoe Store in Alexandria Bay. Folino's was an institution for shoes and shoe repairs in the 1000 Islands from 1933 until they closed a few years after Tony Folino, the store's originator, died in 1997. They carried the Sperry Top-Sider brand, which from all accounts was the first boat shoe.

My curiosity had gotten the best of me, and I went to the Internet to get a detailed history. The Sperry Top-Sider story is well documented. Paul Sperry was a sailing enthusiast who sought a solution for maintaining traction on a slippery boat deck. In 1935 he noticed that his Cocker

Spaniel, Prince, had the ability to move around on wet surfaces and even ice without difficulty. He examined the dog's paws and noticed wavy cracks in the tissue. He cut similar herringbone-type grooves into a rubber outsole, which caused the rubber to spread and grip more efficiently when pressure was applied. Sperry boat shoes have flourished, and are currently the official footwear of the U.S. Sailing Team and other high profile boating organizations.

During the 1980s when boat shoes were featured in the "The Official Preppy Handbook" and again in recent years, this footwear has been at the forefront of fashion. While boat shoes have been in and out of fashion with the general public, this unique footwear has had uninterrupted popularity in the 1000 Islands where boating is the central theme. Dew and rain are frequent companions to boating in this region, and non-skid boat shoes have a ready-made niche.

I noted that some folks kick around in worn out models that should have been thrown out decades ago. I still was wearing a pair of Timberlands that were thirty years old. The inserts wore out and were discarded long ago. Nonetheless the stitching looked like new. I had splattered paint on them, and put them through a torture test that would satisfy the most stringent consumer report.

For some there is increased status associated with continuing to wear a pair of this moccasin-type footwear long after the fashion conscious would have banished them to the Thrift Store. In the 1000 Islands even society's upper crust can be seen at upscale functions sporting many of the numerous brands on the market today.

It took time and mental energy to consider the history of each diverse item and to decide what would become its fate. At times I could take no more, and I had to step back and wait another day before resuming work on our daunting project. It was a mind-boggling task deciding where to start and how to proceed. Dozens of bags of sorted trash went to the dump. Countless bags of clothes, shoes, and other household goods went to the Thrift Store.

We gifted some of the historic contents like the ninety-year-old sail-boat *MT* to the Antique Boat Museum along with related racing accessories and memorabilia. We donated boxes of books to the Macsherry Library and gifted some wares and other items to friends. We could have conducted the world's longest-running yard sale had we been motivated to do so.

CHAPTER 65

Buried Treasures

THE PROPERTY DID not sell in 2012 and, in keeping with my promise, Cathy Garlock became our new realtor at the end of June 2013. On September tenth we were away in Lake Placid, in order to avoid dwelling on the fact that it was the day before Coty would have been twenty-eight, when I received a call from Cathy saying a Mr. Stephen Brown had made a serious offer for the property. For the next twenty-four hours, Kira and I considered the proposal, which was higher than the reserve we had set for the ill-fated auction. We accepted the offer, which meant that our casual approach to removing contents a little at a time suddenly had a deadline.

Most of the Alson Clark artwork had already been relocated, and we had gradually removed approximately one hundred large trash bags filled with both wanted and unwanted wares over the previous five years. Now that it was apparent that the house was going to sell in 2013, we realized that the original mountain of work clearing out the contents was still a mountain of work.

The channel side room between the living room and the master bedroom became a convenient spot to store almost anything no one knew what to do with otherwise. It was fondly referred to as the "antique room." Paint cans with little or no paint remaining found a temporary parking place on a cheap set of metal shelves that should have been dropped off at the Thrift Store when the decision was made to bring them to the island instead. Old lamps that had been replaced or no longer worked were tucked in between chairs and small tables that were too dilapidated for further service.

I pondered how the room got its name while my eyes scanned the conglomeration of junk. "Ah yes, there is the likely reason," I said to myself as I focused on the 1880s agitating-washer. Four one-by-four inch boards, three feet long acted as wooden legs supporting a rustic wooden tub. The top was included a hinged door for inserting and removing clothes. A corrugated sheet of metal sealed the bottom while a flywheel and handle were affixed to the side of this early ancestor of modern home appliances. The flywheel drove a cog that spun what looked like a suspended footstool back and forth inside the tub. The clever device was effective because the five rounded wooden pegs of the footstool-like apparatus swirled the clothes around in the soapy water.

In short, this room was so full of assorted clutter that it was difficult getting the door open much less move around inside the room. The two closets were filled full-to-overflowing, and the last time we had made any attempt to access this space was during a 2009 visit by a group representing the Alexandria Township Historical Society that included Rhea Arnot and Trish Tague. Susie Smith joined the scavenger hunt in order to file a firsthand report on the upcoming exhibit in her capacity as the editor of Thousand Islands Life magazine. They had come to see what relevant river related artwork was at Comfort Island. We had agreed to loan materials for the 2009 - 2010 exhibit featuring my great uncle, Alson S. Clark. As I dug my way through one obstacle after another, I gained an appreciation for what it might be like to return to a dwelling after a tornado had deposited a houseful of belongings into one surviving room.

Our visitors were aware that some of my great uncle's paintings were quite valuable, and they made comments like, "You have got be kidding" as I pulled another landscape oil painting from the recesses of a closet or found a couple tucked in a corner behind a trunk. In addition to paintings I found an assortment of his sketchbooks, an easel, pigments and even one of his palettes.

I was sifting through a box where I'd found a couple of sketchbooks when I pulled a letter out and scanned the subject matter. It was a letter thanking my grandfather for lending a pair of binoculars to the United States Navy during World War I. I looked twice when I got to the closing, which had been personally signed by the Secretary of the Navy, Franklin

D. Roosevelt. I suppose it was no coincidence that the binoculars in question had been returned and were in a leather case on a wicker table next to the front door.

In July 2011 the *Moonrise Kingdom* crew brought back several tons of contents in boxes and in cardboard sleeves that were designed to protect photos, mirrors and paintings. If you guessed that they deposited most of the jumbled mess in the antique room, you are right.

With only a couple of weeks remaining before the sale closed, I reluctantly tackled the antique room being unable to avoid it any longer. I felt dismay and then panic as I sorted through boxes stuffed with thousands of photos, letters, and other scraps of history. I rued the reality of living in a mansion. I questioned how one room and two walk-in closets could possibly hold that many possessions?

It took several days before I accepted the fact that visual and mental overload had taken over and I could sort no more. I collected a myriad of items I wanted to scrutinize at a more leisurely pace, and I put those items into boxes that we then transported to our shared family home on Grenadier Island. Surely I left a few treasures behind, but I'm also excited about the prospect of enjoying the curious antiquities I expect to discover.

As for the treasures that we missed during the final sorting, I'm pleased to share the riches with a new steward who shows so much potential as a kindred spirit!

CHAPTER 66

"River Rats"

THE IROQUOIS INDIANS dubbed the 1000 Islands region as "Manatoana" or the "Garden of the Great Spirit," but I'm not sure they expected that the region's wildlife symbol would one day be an aquatic member of the rodent family named a "muskrat." I would find the critters more visually attractive if it weren't for their tails that look too much like the rat that wriggled by me when I opened the water-heater enclosure back in Florida.

People who spend inordinate amounts of time on the river and hold it in a revered position proudly wear the colloquial mantle of "being a river rat." I count myself as a member of the river rat society even though it has no formal designation and it is surely not a club, but there is a magical quality to the river that draws me back each spring and makes me sorry to leave in the fall. There is a beguiling element to the river setting that defies being controlled or possessed. A gentle breeze and the therapeutic aroma of pine needles are forever etched in my memory on that section of the flagstone path to the house where it passes the post that supported the ancient yard-light. The sound of Herons and Ospreys contesting the territory close to the Osprey nesting site across the channel is haunting and unforgettable. Each season I have checked to see if the wren family will continue to produce young and make their home in the corner post at the edge of the dining porch.

Special venues are produced one event at a time, and Comfort Island has been one of those settings that produced a parade of memorable experiences on an ongoing basis for six generations of Clarks. We rejoice to think that the new owner has roots in the 1000 Islands, and he demonstrates characteristics that convince me that he is already a fellow river rat. I see promise that he will create his own distinctive version of special happenings and memories for his friends and family at Comfort Island in the years to come.

My intent was to find someone who would feel a kinship for the history and grandeur of the Victorian setting. Mr. Brown talks about adding a bell tower and upgrading the porch outside the channel side bedroom. Preserving the murals will require bringing a specialist from Chicago to tackle that challenge.

I think back on Bob Schleinig's comment relative to the movie industry and how the *Moonrise Kingdom* team overcame knotty obstacles within minutes. He said, "All it takes is lots of money."

Comfort's new owner is on the positive end of the financial spectrum with funds to upgrade, whereas we were struggling to simply keep the operation afloat while the premises declined. It is exciting to think about what it would be like taking on some of the projects Mr. Brown contemplates. Comfort Island may yet return those former days of magnificence. One thing is sure: the view, the beach, and the overall location continues to rival any place on earth.

CHAPTER 67

—— ✂ ——

How Does One Say Goodbye
to a Place so Dear?

KIRA AND I were charter members of the Comfort Island unpaid help team. Peter Henderson joined the team in 1993, and he was pivotal in establishing the "Home Depot" restoration program. At some point in the 1980s I instituted the catch-and-release program for wayward bats that chose to roam the entire house rather than confining their activity to the attic. This program went high-tech in 1996 when John Butts, the proprietor of Roscoe Incorporated fishing tackle, presented me with a state of the art "bat net."

I have few regrets in moving on. I feel Kira and I did our best to keep the Clark presence at Comfort Island going as long as it made sense to the very last person involved, which in this case was me. It was a colossal project for anyone to take on, and Kira, Deb, Ellen-Betsy and I took it on for more than thirty years after Dad demonstrated his unending fondness for the "forsaken acres" theme.

I've seen families who hung on to islands they couldn't afford until their financial ship was going down, and some of these folks went down with that ship. We may have hung on to Comfort when it no longer made sense, but I consider it time and money well spent as I reflect on the special memories and the unique heritage six generations of Clarks shared together.

I have been blessed to have a wife who is as dedicated and connected to the river as I am. She, her cousin George, and George's dad Bud played important roles in this story with "a happy ending," since they paved the way for us to simply move a few miles downriver to another superlative setting now that Comfort Island has moved into new hands.

Saying goodbye to such a precious part of my heritage is difficult, but as I say goodbye, I know that I did my best to insure that this magical setting lives on as a venue that approaches the form that Great Grandmother and Great Grandfather Clark intended. The passing of Mamie Clark provided the impetus to take up residency at Comfort Island and ironically the death of Coty Clark sealed our resolve to end a Clark tenancy that lasted 131 years.

Goodbye Dear Comfort. May you flourish again in the years to come.

TAD CLARK WAS born and raised in Southern California. A teenager when he spent his first summer at the treasured family home on Comfort Island in Upstate New York, he went on to marry a river girl. They raised children and grandchildren who continue to make the journey from their current residence in Asheville, North Carolina, to the Thousand Islands each summer. Over the years, Clark has written numerous articles about this scenic archipelago on the Saint Lawrence River.

Made in the USA
Lexington, KY
15 February 2017